Introduction

ire is a capricious friend. One moment it can be
the best companion imaginable. An instant later it can turn
on you with a vengeance.

I think back to a camping trip with my husband a
number of years ago. For weeks on end I had looked forward to spending a cold evening huddled alongside a
warm fire in the high Sierras. *That* is living! That's why I
didn't mind when Ken left me by the fire pit one night to
fill his canteen at the creek.

It was such a pleasant summer night. The stars
seemed to hang low—like the lower lights on a Christmas

tree—in a broad sweep of sky overhead. A slight breeze wafted the scent of pine right into our camp, and the fire cracked and popped with amiable conversation. I sat mesmerized in front of the orange-red coals, feeling the heat on my cheeks, breathing in an aroma of burning oak.

The fire was my friend in the middle of a dark, cold forest.

Suddenly a wind came up and the whole picture changed. In an instant, the flames vaulted higher and a choking cloud of smoke enveloped me. Unable to wheel myself away from the fire—or even cry out—I could only sit there, sputtering and coughing. Terrified, I watched the growing flames begin to lick around my feet. For a few awful seconds, I was afraid I would be seriously burned—and there was nothing I could do about it.

At that moment Ken returned, dropped his canteen, and ran to push my wheelchair out of the path of smoke and fire. There was no harm done, but I gained a new respect for our campfire that night. I learned how quickly a cozy mountain blaze can turn from friend to foe.

Fire. It's another one of those things with great potential for good—and equal potential for hurt and harm. A campfire can barbecue tasty hamburgers one moment only to break its boundaries and attack a forest the next.

So it is with suffering.

With profound potential for good, it can also be a destroyer. Suffering can pull marriages and families together, uniting them through hardship, or it can rip them apart in selfishness and bitterness. Suffering can file all the rough edges off your character, or it can harden your heart like iron.

It all depends.

On us.

On how we respond.

It depends on what we choose to do in the middle of our suffering. Do we use it—or let it use us? Do we go to God, or try to battle it on our own?

James has a good word for us when trials comes sweeping over our horizon like a Kansas twister: "Blessed is the man who remains steadfast under trial, for when he has stood the test he will receive the crown of life, which God has promised to those who love him" (James 1:12, ESV).

Adversity, which looks and feels like such a deter-mined enemy, can become a valuable ally.

Only you can decide which it will be.

If you aren't experiencing adversity at this moment, then I will be a prophet to you: It will come. It's as much a part of life on this broken planet as sunrise and sunset, as wind in the trees. But God has given us the power to *choose* what we do with it.

Join me, dear reader, through thirty-one days of thoughts, Scriptures, prayers, and specific ideas for overcoming and living above our adversities. If you have the opportunity, travel this monthlong passage with your spouse or a friend, because we all know that troubles shared are troubles halved. If no one comes to mind, then let me be that friend to you. We'll walk together, you and I. I would like that very much.

Like you, I have tasted the bitter waters of adversity in my life.

Only a God like ours can show us the sweet, hidden springs of an overcoming life.

Day 1

WE MAY ASK WHY

*I*f the Lord Jesus cried out on His cross, "My God, my God, why have you forsaken me?" is it okay for me to ask the question "Why?"

I wondered that for the longest time. My cries of "Why, God, why?" weren't voiced out of anger. For the most part, it was just a human cry of desperation, out of my own agony.

Over the years I've discovered it's no sin to ask the Lord why things happen. God can handle our questions. But here's the important thing: *Can we handle His answers?*

Yes, there are answers. But many of us get so caught up in asking "Why me?" that we forget about seeking those answers. The fact is, we may not like them. They may be hard to swallow. But we can't ignore the truth that God can and often does give crystal clear answers to our heart's deepest questions.

So why has God allowed the hurt you're facing today? You might find part of your answer in the words of Peter:

> Dear friends, do not be surprised at the painful trial you are suffering, as though something strange were happening to you. But rejoice that you may participate in the sufferings of Christ, so that you may be overjoyed when his glory is revealed.
>
> 1 PETER 4:12–13

You see, part of the answer to the "whys" you are asking might be that God wants you to have a small share in the sort of suffering your Savior went through.

Paul echoes a similar thought:

> Now if we are children, then we are heirs—heirs of God and co-heirs with Christ, if indeed we

share in his sufferings in order that we may also
share in his glory.

ROMANS 8:17

Once again God gives us at least a partial answer to
our "why" questions. It's almost as though God is saying
to us, *Why not?* If Jesus went through so much...so much
suffering and heartache to secure for us that which we
don't deserve...if He went through the pain, why should
we complain if we have to endure a tiny part of what He
endured on our behalf?

The Bible makes it clear that suffering is mysteriously
and intimately linked with the glory that lies beyond. The
Bible passages we considered today remind us we can
rejoice over the privilege of participating in the sufferings
of Christ—so that we will be overjoyed when we share in
His glory to come.

Granted, that may not be anything close to the kind of
answer we want or expect to the questions we ask of God.
But God's not the one who has to prove Himself here.

You've been more than ready to ask the questions.
The real issue is, will you accept His answers?

Wayside Interlude

"I'm speechless, in awe—words fail me.
I should never have opened my mouth!
I've talked too much, way too much.
I'm ready to shut up and listen."

JOB 40:4–5, *THE MESSAGE*

As a result, I can really know Christ and experience the mighty power that raised him from the dead. I can learn what it means to suffer with him, sharing in his death, so that, somehow, I can experience the resurrection from the dead!

PHILIPPIANS 3:10–11, NLT

Before you can accept God's answers, you first must hear them. You must allow Him time and opportunity to respond to your questions. He has promised wisdom to those who ask (James 1:5), but don't expect Him to shout or leave a text message on your cell phone. He will speak into the stillness of a quiet, listening, seeking heart.

Day 2

OUR SUFFERING...
AND HIS

*I*t's no use trying to fake it with the staff at Joni and Friends. They've seen me at my worst.

On different occasions I've come into the office downcast, completely disheartened for one reason or another. My friends in our ministry have had the sensitivity to be a real comfort to me. After sharing a few mutual problems and prayer needs, I begin to feel like I honestly *am* a part of the fellowship of suffering.

All Christians participate in that marvelous fellowship.

Through the smiles, sharing of struggles, prayerful lifting of burdens, tears, and even the consolation and occasional advice, we are initiated into the fellowship of Christ's sufferings.

For all believers, there is a wonderful, inexplicable participation in the life and power of Jesus when we suffer. Ours is a fellowship in which the power of Jesus is made perfect, not just alongside or beyond our weaknesses, but actually *in* our weaknesses. Two of the words most associated with Christians in their suffering are *comfort* and *joy*.

But it's right at this point that we need to understand a big difference between *our* suffering and the suffering our Lord endured.

For the Lord Jesus, there was no fellowship in suffering. For Him, there was only the wooden insensitivity of His disciples—from the first day right up to the end of His ministry. For Him, there was only that awful climax of isolation on the cross, even to the point of being forsaken by the Father and abandoned to God's blazing wrath.

There was no real *joy* in His cross as there can be in ours. Hebrews 12:2 tells us that "for the joy *set before him*

[he] endured the cross." In other words, Jesus focused on that which was beyond those ghastly hours: on His future back with the Father, and on the salvation of millions who would trust Him through history. But thankfully for us, we can have joy *in* our affliction. Right in the heart of it. Ours is a comfort we can experience *now* as we suffer.

For Jesus, it was a different story. Far different. And His story was the way it was, so that your story might be the way it could be. You don't have to be alone in your hurt. Comfort *is* yours! Joy *is* an option. And it's all been made possible by your Savior. As someone once said...

He went without comfort so that
you might have it.
He postponed joy so that you might share in it.
He willingly chose isolation so that you might
never be alone.
He had no real fellowship so that fellowship might
be yours, this moment.

So let's you and I drop our martyr complex, okay? You will never experience isolation or abandonment or the dread of being forsaken as did your Lord. Fellowship is yours! The fellowship of suffering!

And you have it because He didn't.

Wayside Interlude

But it was our sins that did that to him,
that ripped and tore and crushed him—our sins!
He took the punishment, and that made us whole.
Through his bruises we get healed.

ISAIAH 53:5, THE MESSAGE

Difficult circumstances in our lives can either drive a wedge between us and our Savior…or drive us deeper into the comfort of His embrace. We can isolate ourselves, withdrawing from sustaining relationships with fellow believers, or we can seek the prayers, counsel, and encouragement of a few close friends in Christ. One path will add loneliness on top of our sorrows; the other will provide comfort as deep as our need.

OUR BODIES, LIKE TENTS

When we went beach camping as kids, I thought living in a tent was the ultimate adventure.

Sand on the canvas floor? Who cares? Mosquitoes? Just get out the mosquito netting. Rain? Break out the tarps and pull down the canvas flaps. Dirt? Well, my goodness, a little dirt never hurt anybody.

I thought living in a tent was great fun. I could have done it all summer.

Now, decades later, it's a different story. Ken and I still enjoy camping, but I can only take it for so long. For some reason, tent camping seems to get a little more strenuous with each passing year. Sand, mosquitoes, dirt, rain? *You can have it,* I say to myself after four or five days.

Maybe that's why the apostle Paul (himself a part-time tentmaker) likened living in these bodies of ours to living in a tent.

A tent is only temporary. We can only take it for so long. And with each passing year, we find living in these bodies of ours more strenuous than the year before.

Aren't you glad we won't always be "groaning and burdened" with these patchwork tents of ours, as Paul says in 2 Corinthians 5:4?

When I think along these lines, Steve Coyle's story comes to mind. Fit and strong, Steve swam for an hour each morning. One day a diving accident badly bruised his spinal column. He recovered from that mishap, but just three months later had another accident which left him a quadriplegic. Even so, Steve never complained about his disability. He always managed to work in some words of praise to the Lord in all his conversation.

I wish the story got better from there, but the truth is, Steve then developed cancer. He suffered greatly, and after losing over eighty pounds, he went to be with the Lord. How he must have grown weary of his tent!

Shortly before he died, Steve wanted to record some of his thoughts in verse. He entrusted these lines to a nurse friend.

When I looked upon the days gone past,
    I'd thought this tent was built to last.
For I'd stood it on some rocky ground
    where stormy winds couldn't beat it down.
And with my pride and my own hand,
    I put my tent on shifting sand
where pegs pulled loose and my tent did shake,
    but I was young and I could take
the unstable world that I was in;
    I'd just up and move again.
So for many years I went this route,
    shifting this old tent about.
Till one cold day when my mind grew clear,
    this tent had an end and it might be near.

So with much fear (such a heavy load)
    I looked for the One who made this abode.
Yes, the Tentmaker, He'd surely know
    where one such rotting tent should go
to have this canvas revitalized,
    to have these poles and pegs resized.
I went to Him on bended knees
    begging Him, "Oh Tentmaker, please!
Restore this tent I thought would last,
    this canvas house that went so fast."
He looked at me through loving eyes
    and merely pointed to the skies.
"Please don't grieve over some old tent,
    old canvas walls that have been spent.
For this mansion that's been built by Me
    will last you for eternity."

With that assurance, Steve Coyle gladly broke camp
and moved on.

Wayside Interlude

For instance, we know that when these bodies of
ours are taken down like tents and folded away,
they will be replaced by resurrection bodies in
heaven—God-made, not handmade—and we'll
never have to relocate our "tents" again.

2 CORINTHIANS 5:1–3, *THE MESSAGE*

*Taking down a tent after a week of camping is a prospect as
happy as setting it up at the beginning of the week. The adventure
may have been fun, but a hot shower awaits! And a real bed with
clean sheets and all the comforts of home. Take some time to pon-
der the comforts of your eternal home—waiting for you as soon as
you set aside this temporary tent.*

THRESHING

*M*y friend took a unique vacation lately. Shunning Disneyland and the High Sierras, she, her husband, and their kids drove back to the family farm in North Dakota to help with the wheat harvest. Can you imagine? Hundreds of acres of wheat under a wide-open sky. Big combine tractors. An old farmhouse. A towering windmill. Doesn't it sound like fun? Actually, as Bev recounted their experiences, she reminded me that it was a lot of work...but good, hard, family-fun work.

Since I didn't know much about wheat, I asked her to describe just what goes on at harvest. Bev recounted how the big combines come lumbering through the fields, raking the furrows of freshly cut wheat into the machine. The combine head, which resembles a rotating blade, then beats or *threshes* the stalks of wheat. The ripe grain is shaken loose and sucked into a large bin at the back of the combine. What's left, the straw and the chaff, goes back onto the ground, fodder for the next gust of prairie wind.

Since my conversation with Bev, I've learned that the biblical word *tribulation* has its root meaning in the word *thresh*. What I've just described to you, believe it or not, is a process that applies to believers as well as wheat.

In Romans 5:3, Paul tells us that "suffering produces perseverance." If I were to sit down with you today over a cup of coffee, I have a feeling you could put very personal words around that experience. A few of those big combines have most likely rumbled across the field toward you within the past year. Perhaps within the past *week*.

Adversities. Those big unavoidable trials that threaten to cut you down and beat you back and forth. Being threshed is never easy. Never pleasant. But Romans 5 goes on to assure us that perseverance, the fruit of tribulation, yields a crop of proven character (vv. 3–4).

God is after something precious in your soul. Just as with that North Dakota farmer, He's after a harvest—the golden grain of patience, perseverance, and strong character. And how is that grain harvested? Only through threshing. Through adversity. The farmer doesn't thresh weeds, does he? He wouldn't waste his time. He threshes the wheat which yields grain from the chaff. That priceless, blessed grain.

I know it's hard to picture the "results" or the "yield" when you're going through so much testing. It's hard to imagine how God might be pleased or how you might be benefited. But splendid spiritual grain is to be found only in the lives of those with noble character—character gleaned through threshing.

Shortly before His betrayal and death on the cross, the Lord Jesus turned to Peter and said, "Simon, Simon, Satan has asked to sift you as wheat. But I have prayed for you, Simon, that your faith may not fail. And when you have turned back, strengthen your brothers" (Luke 22:31).

Jesus predicted that Peter was about to get mowed down by one big threshing machine of a trial. Yet the Lord never said He would pluck Simon out of the path of that trial, only that He would pray that Simon's faith would not fail—in spite of the threshing. Christ was after lasting fruit in Simon's life—patience, yes, but perseverance even more so.

"You did not choose me," Jesus said in John 15:16, "but I chose you...to go and bear fruit—fruit that will last." I'm glad that the grain, the fruit in our lives, will last.

Somehow that makes the beating and the flailing of a threshing trial worthwhile.

Wayside Interlude

Dear brothers and sisters, whenever trouble comes your way, let it be an opportunity for joy. For when your faith is tested, your endurance has a chance to grow. So let it grow, for when your endurance is fully developed, you will be strong in character and ready for anything.

JAMES 1:2–4, NLT

No discipline is enjoyable while it is happening—it is painful! But afterward there will be a quiet harvest of right living for those who are trained in this way.

HEBREWS 12:11, NLT

When we're in the middle of adversity, it feels all consuming. Faith flickers, hope falters, courage burns low. It sometimes seems as if the dark times will never end. And these are the hours when the enemy of our soul whispers his lies of discouragement and despair. Jesus told Peter a better day would be coming after the crisis that would nearly crush him. He would return to strength, encouragement, and the light of a new day. We, too, need the perspective and counsel of Jesus in our trials. Seek Him now. Spread all your life out before Him. Wait on Him to bring forth a good and glad harvest in your life, as He promised.

He Cares for You

Cast all your anxiety on him because he cares for you.

1 PETER 5:7

hat's not only a fragment of Scripture, it's a *foundation* of Scripture. God's acts of compassion and mercy never go unnoticed by the authors of the Bible. Time and again, God demonstrates His love through this intimate, very personal care of His children.

Some carry this idea even further. God cares so much for us, these individuals say, that He would never want *any* hurt or heartache to touch our lives.

"If we really had faith," they reason, "if we really trusted in Him, God would go to any length to release us from our pain."

While no one is saying God enjoys watching our struggles, Scripture clearly indicates that He allows certain wounds and hardships to prick and pierce our lives. But it never means He no longer cares.

God certainly cared for Timothy, who struggled with frequent illness. He cared for James, the brother of John, who was cut down by a sword because of his testimony. He cared for John, exiled and isolated on a lonely island.

God's care for all these people was not inconsistent with the fact of their suffering. Hebrews 12:6 tells us "the Lord disciplines those he loves."

As Paul sat in a Jerusalem prison cell, the Lord kindly appeared to him and said, "Take heart! —for as you have witnessed boldly for me in Jerusalem so you must give your witness for me in Rome" (Acts 23:11, *Phillips*).

God cared about Paul. And no doubt Paul took his friend Peter's advice and cast all his anxiety upon God. Even so...he remained in custody for at least *two years* after the Lord appeared to him that night. Did God stop caring during those two years? Of course not. God answered His servant's prayer by giving him the kind of peace which allowed him to write, "I have learned to be content, whatever the circumstances may be. I know now how to live when things are difficult and I know how to live when things are prosperous. In general and in particular I have learned the secret of eating well or going hungry—of facing either plenty or poverty. I am ready for anything through the strength of the One who lives within me" (Philippians 4:11–13, *Phillips*).

He cares for you.

It's a beautiful promise that reminds you of God's intimate concern whether you're ill for days, unemployed for weeks, disabled for months, or struggling with your marriage for years.

Grab hold of that truth and hang on. No matter what.

Wayside Interlude

Give your burdens to the Lord. He will carry
them. He will not permit the godly to slip or fall.

PSALM 55:22, TLB

*What does it really mean to "cast your cares" on the Lord, or
to give your burdens to Him? Have you ever been backpacking?
There's nothing quite like the feeling of taking a break along the
trail and slipping that heavy weight off your aching shoulders for a
few minutes. Our Lord invites us to do just that. As we pray, as we
consider Him, worship Him, and walk with Him, He wants us to
slip the weight off of our shoulders — to consciously loosen the
straps and allow Him to lift it from us. Do it now! Don't let the
weight of anxieties, worries, and disappointments cut into your
shoulders and steal your joy.*

GOD'S DETAILED ARTWORK

One of the reasons I so love my artwork is that often God uses it to surprise me with some flash of insight, some fresh way of looking at His word.

That happened to me a number of years ago when I was working on a rendering of the face of the virgin Mary for a Christmas design. She had to look like a young Jewish peasant, but I wanted to depict her in such a way that her royalty and nobility would shine right out of her face.

I gathered all kinds of photos of young Jewish women. I pored over fashion magazines to scrutinize cheekbones. I experimented with cool and hot and warm pinks. I even did a study of eyebrows. Then came revision after revision, erasure after erasure, test after test.

Poor Mary. I put her face through everything, trying to attain the perfect, the ideal, the best rendering for the final painting.

It's easy to set aside sketches I care little about or ideas that don't particularly excite me. I can even endure a slight mistake or two. But when I get truly excited about a piece, believe me, it gets bruised and battered with erasures and revisions. I push that rendering until it's just what I envision.

I'm convinced God deals with us in the same way. For us to ask God to leave us alone or stop refining us is to ask Him to love us less, not more.

Many of us think God "unloving" when He puts us through the test, pulling and pushing us, changing us into that complete idea of who He wants us to be. Could it be we're only considering a single dimension of His love — say, kindness, or gentleness—and blowing it up as if it were the whole thing?

God's love is deeper and wider than that. It embraces constructive criticism, admonishment, correction, and spurring a person to do his or her best. If by love we mean keeping another from suffering or discomfort, then we say that God is not always loving. Neither is a doctor who sticks a needle into the bottom of a crying infant.

We are the objects of God's profound love and attention. Don't ask Him to stop perfecting and improving you. God has a final idea in mind and He's bringing you into completion—through revision after revision, erasure after erasure, sketch after sketch.

By doing that, He's not loving you less. Believe me, He's loving you more.

Wayside Interlude

God knew what he was doing from the very beginning. He decided from the outset to shape the lives of those who love him along the same lines as the life of his Son.

ROMANS 8:29, *THE MESSAGE*

There is no such thing as "random suffering" in the life of a child of God. Our sovereign God is a God of intent and purpose. He never does things capriciously! This means our trials and adversities—difficult, perplexing, and heartbreaking as they might be at times—are never "senseless." God's great purpose and plan for each of our lives embraces everything from minor irritations to devastating losses and setbacks. Let the prayer of David be yours today—all day long.

> *But I trust in you, O LORD; I say,*
> *"You are my God."*
> *My times are in your hands.*

PSALM 31:14–15

TEARS

*M*any years ago, when I was a teenager in the hospital, I noticed something very peculiar. Even though there was so much pain, so much disappointment in the lives of kids my age who were rehabilitating from accidents and injuries—even though you knew they were hurting—no one cried.

Sometimes I would lie awake in the middle of the night in my hospital room. I was so near tears, but I fought them back. For one thing, there was no one around to blow my nose or wipe my eyes. But I was also afraid. Afraid I would wake up my roommates and they would hear me. Maybe, just maybe, they would make fun of me the next day at physical therapy. So I kept my tears to myself.

That reminds me of something Chuck Colson once told me. "Men and women in prison don't cry," he said. "It's a sign of weakness, and weakness can be dangerous in prison."

Thankfully, things changed once I got out of that hospital and got my act together with the Lord. Getting closer to Jesus taught me weakness was something to boast in, something to delight in. Even the apostle Paul, who told us he gloried in his weakness, wrote to the Corinthian church with "much anguish of heart and many tears" (2 Corinthians 2:4).

Then I learned about David—a real man's man, a warrior, and a king. He cried, too. The pages of the psalms are salted with this man's tears. In Hebrews I read of Jesus offering prayers and petitions "with loud cries and tears" (Hebrews 5:7).

Big, burly Peter demonstrated that tears are only natural when one feels remorse or regret—like the time he heard the rooster crow a second time, recognized his sin, and wept bitterly.

Learning about these people in Scripture gave me the courage and confidence to cry! No longer were tears an embarrassment, a mark of weakness or shame.

What do your tears mean to you? The Bible tells us that "those who sow in tears will reap with songs of joy" (Psalm 126:5). God gives you a reason to hope, even though you find it tough to hold back the tears. Weeping won't last forever. But out of your grief, love, or repentance, God brings a peace that *does* last forever.

Revelation 7:17 puts it this way: "For the Lamb at the center of the throne will be their shepherd; he will lead them to springs of living water. And God will wipe away every tear from their eyes."

It's ironic. In heaven, where I will be able once again to wipe my own tears, I won't have to.

Wayside Interlude

Hear my prayer, O LORD, and give ear to my cry;
    hold not your peace at my tears!
For I am a sojourner with you,
    a guest, like all my fathers.

PSALM 39:12, ESV

Happy are those who are strong in the Lord, who
want above all else to follow your steps. When
they walk through the Valley of Weeping, it will
become a place of springs where pools of blessing
and refreshment collect after rains!

PSALM 84:5–6, TLB

Praise the Lord with me: *We praise You, our great God
and Savior, that not a single tear that slips from our eyes goes
unnoticed by You. Hallelujah! We can't begin to understand why
You should involve Yourself so intimately in our lives, or care so
deeply about our heartaches and concerns. Yet by faith in this very
moment, we believe and accept that You do. We yearn for the day
when Your own tender hand, Lord, will wipe away our tears forever.*

Day 8

HALFWAY HOME

I've seen him in the hills above town, early in the morning, running in line with his high school teammates.

Most days after school Clay does volunteer work at our office, packing boxes and stuffing envelopes. But now that it's cross-country season, he's out on the roads and trails, pushing his body to its limits.

Keeping me updated, my young friend tells me that his school has already won several meets this year. In one race, he placed tenth in a field of sixty-five harriers.

When I had the chance, I asked Clay a question that

had been on my mind since he joined the team: *What's the most difficult part of a long-distance run?*

I've heard some say it's that first mile or so. Your muscles feel tight and the long course seems to stretch out forever before you. Others have told me it's that final stretch that's the killer. You're exhausted, your limbs feel like wood, and you're scarcely able to lift one foot in front of the other.

But Clay had a different answer. The worst part of a cross-country run, he told me, is neither the beginning nor the end. It's the middle — the long and lonely tramp, those seemingly endless minutes when you're out of the range of those cheering voices at the start and finish lines. It's that long, gray, middle distance that saps your strength and your will.

My friend quoted a verse that helps him when he hits that midpoint in the race.

Those who hope in the LORD will renew their strength…they will run and not grow weary, they will walk and not be faint.

ISAIAH 40:31

$$\mathscr{D}ay\ 8$$

Some say the prophet Isaiah had those very midpoint blues in mind when he gave this prophecy to Israel. As Israel was released at last from the long captivity, God promised He would go with them on the long trek from Babylon to Jerusalem. And yes, He would be with them when they hit that desolate midpoint of the journey…when the way back was as far as the way forward…when the desert sun washed the landscape of color and the destination seemed a lost and distant thing. A mirage on the far horizon.

Have you been there?

Do you ever feel like you're in the middle of a long stretch of the same old routine? Yes, the beginning of the Christian life was exhilarating. Lots of smiles and handshakes and encouragement. Your emotions soared. And the end? Well, it's going to be indescribably joyous and exciting meeting the Lord Jesus face-to-face.

But now…you're in the middle.

There are miles behind you and, for all you know, miles to go. You don't hear any cheers or applause. That first shot of spiritual adrenaline wore off a long time ago. The days run together. So do the weeks. Your commitment to simply keep putting one tired foot in front of the other begins to flag and fade.

Ah, but the promise in Isaiah is as much for you as it is for Israel. And it is every bit as true now as it was when it was penned thousands of years ago. If we walk in the Spirit, our strength *will* be renewed. We will run and not be weary. Even in the long, gray, middle distance, we will walk and not faint.

The writer of Hebrews also had some good words for fainting saints. In chapter 12 he wrote: "Let us throw off everything that hinders and the sin that so easily entangles, and let us run with perseverance the race marked out for us. Let us fix our eyes on Jesus, the author and perfecter of our faith" (vv. 1–2).

A little later in the chapter he offered some encouragement for those with sore legs and feet—those who seemed on the verge of dropping out of the race: "Therefore, strengthen your feeble arms and weak knees. 'Make level paths for your feet,' so that the lame may not be disabled, but rather healed" (vv. 12–13).

Even though it may not seem like it right now, the race will soon be over. The tape is just ahead—around the bend, over the hill, and through some trees. Believers who have gone ahead crowd the grandstand, awaiting your triumphant finish.

Yes, the middle part of the race is difficult. Sometimes excruciating. But every step brings you closer to that finish line. Fix your eyes on the One who awaits you there.

You're halfway home.

Wayside Interlude

However, I consider my life worth nothing to me,
if only I may finish the race and complete the task
the Lord Jesus has given me—the task of testifying to the gospel of God's grace.

ACTS 20:24

For you have need of endurance, so that when you
have done the will of God, you may receive what
was promised.

HEBREWS 10:36, NASB

Please pray with me: *Father, though our lives here on earth are brief, the way can seem long sometimes. Our bodies become weary, our loads feel heavy, and our strength and hope can fail us just when we need it most. Father, You are the One who promises new strength to the weary. You are the One who lifts our head, and draws us toward the light and beauty just over the horizon. Keep us running strong and steady and true. Refocus our eyes on the Lord Jesus, the One who endured so much for us, and waits for us at the finish line. In His strong name, amen.*

PARTAKERS IN CHRIST

onna Rutley was a senior when I was a lowly freshman, but she took the time to invite me to a high school Young Life meeting. Donna was a Christian and everybody knew it and admired her for it. She was involved in high school clubs, student government, sports, and to me she seemed to move through the halls with her feet inches above the floor. A classic blond-haired, blue-eyed beauty, she seemed oblivious to her good looks, choosing not to spend her break times primping in front of the girls' room mirror, but instead reaching out to new kids in the hall like me.

I studied her. Admired her. Mimicked her mannerisms and copied her style. I tried hard to be a miniature Donna Rutley. *I was going to do my best to be like her.* That smile, that hairstyle, those sorority sweaters and circle pins, her cute expressions—anything to be like Donna.

When I was a senior, long after Donna had graduated, I realized something. I never got to know Donna Rutley. I knew things *about* her, but I didn't *know* her. We'd rarely talked. I knew nothing of her home and family, goals and dreams. And I've no idea at all where she is today. She might have gone on to be a homemaker. Or beauty queen. Or TV announcer. She might already be in heaven. Though I worshiped her from afar, she stepped out of my life, completely and permanently. Yet as I think back on those memories, I realize Donna Rutley taught me a spiritual lesson I'll never forget.

It's not enough to do our best to be like Christ.

To "be like Christ" does not mean we copy His lifestyle or mimic His mannerisms, trying our best to be patient and tolerant, loving and kind. To "be like Christ" is to partake of His very nature.

The writer of Hebrews tells us that we "are made partakers of Christ" and should be "partakers of his holiness" (Hebrews 3:14; 12:10, KJV). Peter tells us that through God's promises we can be partakers of His divine nature (2 Peter 1:4).

Those thoughts sparked my curiosity. I looked up the word *partakers* in the dictionary and found that partakers are people who "take part in, who have a share or a portion of something."

As we see from Scripture, you and I as Christians have a share or a portion of the life of Jesus Christ.

The sufferings we encounter in life—even the garden-variety sort of daily trials—are meant to *help* us partake of Christ. For when we enter the fellowship of His sufferings, God strips us of our "self-help" mindset. We are forced to our knees and driven to lean on His grace. Then—and, it seems, only then—can God impart His Son's character to us. In so doing, we are "made like Him."

When I struggle with this wheelchair, for instance, or during my recent long bout with pneumonia, *I can become more like Christ if I respond rightly.*

I don't become more like Jesus through some positive-thinking, self-help approach. I don't become more sensitive or patient through a hang-in-there, stick-to-it, pull-yourself-up-by-your-bootstraps way of looking at hardships.

No, we don't build up Christ's character in our own lives. He takes responsibility for building us when we become partakers of Him. All of my flesh efforts—my teeth-gritted determination—have nothing to do with becoming more like Jesus. It's only when I partake of Him, when I share His life, read His Word, abide in His presence, converse with Him in prayer, seek His counsel, and delight in His fellowship that I become more like Christ in my sufferings.

Now, we've all been caught "trying our best" to be more patient or sweet-spirited in some given trial. But maybe we ought to concentrate all of that effort on simply being partakers of Jesus. Then we can leave to Him the whole process of being made more like Christ. For as we partake of Him, sharing in His nature, it's inevitable that we'll become more like Him.

Wherever you are, Donna Rutley, thanks for the lesson.

Wayside Interlude

I died on the cross with Christ. And my present life is not that of the old "I," but the living Christ within me. The bodily life I now live, I live believing in the Son of God who loved me and sacrificed himself for me.

GALATIANS 2:20, PHILLIPS

Some people fear surrendering their lives to Jesus Christ because of all they will "lose." **Die to myself? What a radical idea. How frightening.** *Yet the greatest issue in this whole transaction is not the life we lose, but the life we gain! We become partakers in the mighty, glorious, majestic-beyond-imagination, eternal life of God's own Son. He lives His life in and through us. He fills us with His Spirit, covers us with His protection, drenches us with His love and favor, and walks with us through our adversities. To lose everything and gain Jesus is no loss at all.*

THOSE "OTHER" PROMISES

*I*t gives us a nice, warm feeling to sing about the promises of God. Some of us have put God's promises on plaques above our fireplace, or stitched them into a needlepoint for the hallway.

Such snug, comforting promises, such as...

"I have come that [you] may have life, and have it to the full."

JOHN 10:10

"…the living God, who gives us richly all things to enjoy."

1 TIMOTHY 6:17, NKJV

"Ask and it will be given to you; seek and you will find."

MATTHEW 7:7

"Ask, and you will receive, that your joy may be full."

JOHN 16:24, NKJV

We gladly claim those promises as believers. We memorize them, meditate on them, and personalize them. And rightly so. God intends us to enter into His promises. But there's a catch. You can't pick and choose. God means for us to embrace *all* His promises—not just some of them. And not all His promises are snug and comfortable.

Some of God's assurances are more easily ignored, aren't they? Especially the ones having to do with pain and hardship. You don't see *those* promises hanging over fireplaces, or stitched in needlepoint, or penned in the back of Bibles. We have a way of sidestepping them. Yet if there's one thing the New Testament promises the people of God, it is suffering and tribulation, trials and chastening and persecution. All of these things are promised to true disciples.

- Everyone who wants to live a godly life in Christ Jesus will be persecuted. (2 Timothy 3:12)
- "Remember...'No servant is greater than his master.' If they persecuted me, they will persecute you also." (John 15:20)
- Consider it pure joy, my brothers, whenever you face trials of many kinds, because you know that the testing of your faith develops perseverance. (James 1:2–3)
- "Blessed are you when people insult you, persecute you and falsely say all kinds of evil against you because of me." (Matthew 5:11)
- "We must go through many hardships to enter the kingdom of God." (Acts 14:22)
- To this you were called, because Christ suffered for you, leaving you an example, that you should follow in his steps. (1 Peter 2:21)

No, we'd rather not "name 'n' claim" *those* promises. You won't find them gracing many living room walls or magnetized to refrigerator doors. Frankly, we'd rather circumvent the suffering. We make every effort to weed out all the discomfort in our lives. We consider trials and disciplines to be rude interruptions in our plans for an easy, comfortable life. We demand miracles of healing and are willing to believe all sorts of wild irrationalities in order to get what we want. We seek to escape the promise of hardship, rather than allowing our Lord to work out His will in our lives through the experience.

I can recall a time when I used to think those promises were more like threats.

Oh sure, the Bible promises a lot of hardship. Well, with friends like that, who needs enemies? If I break my neck at the age of seventeen, what in the world is going to happen to me when I reach twenty or thirty? If this is the way God is going to start out discipling me, then I might as well forget it!

I just expected that my life should be easy—as though that were some kind of inalienable right as a human being. Life was supposed to be comfortable, with distress and trouble mere exceptions to the rule.

Yet I really wanted to be a disciple! I really wanted to follow Christ!

Do you see yourself in that contradiction? If we want to know Christ, a casual glance at the New Testament will tell us that God's Son was made perfect by suffering (Hebrews 2:10). And if the Christ of glory came to His glory only through suffering, how shall we know His glory any other way? If we want to know Him, and if we want to be made like Him, we can expect a few bumps and bruises along the way.

And that's a promise!

Wayside Interlude

"If we are his children then we are God's heirs, and all that Christ inherits will belong to all of us as well! Yes, if we share in his sufferings we shall certainly share in his glory.

ROMANS 8:17, *PHILLIPS*

Please pray with me: *Lord Jesus, the early disciples counted it a great honor to suffer abuse and shame for Your sake. Even as I lean hard on Your promises to save me, keep me, supply for me, and take care of me, Lord, help me to remember that You have NOT promised me freedom from pain, heartache, and loss along the way. May my devotion prove true to You both in the times of testing and the times of ease. In Your sustaining name, amen.*

BEATING THE WAVES

I've always loved the ocean.

I treasure special memories of camping at Bethany Beach in Delaware when I was a girl. The waves would come in over a long sandbar, breaking up to seven feet high, spilling creamy surf over acres of sand.

Now, when you're a child—and I couldn't have been more than six or seven—those waves can look pretty high. When I saw them coming, my first inclination was to swim the other way. But that would be a mistake, because the rolling, foaming surf tosses you every which way, sometimes holding you underneath the water for what seems like forever.

No, I learned that the best thing you could do when those waves swelled was to swim fast *toward* them and dive *under* the wave before it had a chance to break on top of you. You really had to hold your breath as you dove through the wave. But oh, the relief you felt as you broke the surface and could hear that huge great wave breaking behind you. *You had beat the wave,* and it was exhilarating.

Funny how the lessons you learn at a young age stick with you through the years. Because even though I don't dive or swim anymore, I can still "beat the waves."

Waves of crisis or difficulty roll in from the horizon and threaten to break over my life. Looking up at them, they seem so high, so insurmountable. My first inclination is to run the other way, attempting to escape those frightening problems. But there really is no fast escape. Running from problems only tosses me in a foaming fury of entanglements and frustrations and emotions later on.

Jonah learned that lesson in a tough college course called Obedience 101. When he tried to run from the clear

challenge God had laid before him, life became exceed-
ingly complicated. In the inhospitable confines of a fish's
belly, the reluctant prophet reflected on his attempted
escape.

> [Lord,] You hurled me into the deep,
>   into the very heart of the seas,
> and the currents swirled about me;
>   all your waves and breakers swept over me.
>
> The engulfing waters threatened me,
>   the deep surrounded me;
> seaweed was wrapped around my head.
>
> JONAH 2:3, 5

Jonah would agree with me that the best way to beat
those waves of trials and tough challenges is to *face*
them—head-on. Almost anticipating them. Sometimes I
find myself diving into the middle of a problem before it
has a chance to crash on top of me.

And when by God's grace I come through it all? Oh,
the relief when I know that problem is behind me. With

God's help, I've beaten it. What an invigorating feeling!

Well, I'm on my way to a camping trip, so I have to close. I'll sit by the shoreline tonight and watch the waves roll in off the mighty Pacific.

And if only I could swim...I think I might still beat those waves!

Wayside Interlude

I hear the tumult of the raging seas
    as your waves and surging tides sweep over me.
Through each day the LORD pours his unfailing
    love upon me,
and through each night I sing his songs,
    praying to God who gives me life.

PSALM 42:7–8, NLT

What is your greatest challenge or difficulty as you read these words? What looms in front of you as your greatest obstacle? Have you been running from that "wave," allowing your emotions to be tossed and dashed about in the surf? Is there an issue you must deal with eventually, but keep procrastinating? Maybe today is the day to face that wave, and dive right under it in God's strength. What a joy it will be for you to be through that issue, and move on to new challenges and opportunities in Christ!

SURPRISING TRIALS

J admit it: I just can't get used to trials.

Every time I get hit broadside with a fresh dose of trouble, my first response is, "Whoa! Where did *that* come from? God picked *me* to handle this?"

Like the time my van had a flat tire on an LA freeway. And I didn't have my cell phone. My first thought was, *God, You've got the wrong person for this one. Remember? I'm Joni—the lady who's paralyzed from the neck down. I can't exactly hop out, flip open the trunk, grab the jack, and spin on a spare. Good grief, I can't even flag down a passerby or thumb a ride to the local gas station.*

Frankly, I was a little surprised. Or maybe a lot surprised.

I would have thought God could give me a trial more in keeping with my limitations. All I could do was sit helplessly in my van and wait for some kind soul to walk by and give me a hand. (And wait and wait and wait…)

But guess what verse kept floating its way to the top of my thinking?

> Dear friends, do not be surprised at the painful
> trial you are suffering, as though something
> strange were happening to you.
>
> 1 PETER 4:12

I know I've talked a lot about adversity in this little book. But I don't really think I get an unfair share of it. We all encounter troubles and disappointments virtually every day of our lives. But for as many times as I've hit these rough patches in the road, it still comes as a surprise! You'd think I would learn that lesson from reading those verses in First Peter so many times. *"Don't be surprised...as though something strange were happening."*

Apparently, I'm not the only one who can't get used to hardships. Evidently some of Peter's friends couldn't get used to them, either.

But James, Peter's cohort, has some sage advice for people like me (and thee). "Consider it all joy, my brethren, when you encounter various trials, knowing that the testing of your faith produces endurance" (James 1:2–3, NASB).

At first glace that passage seems to say, "Hey, jump up and down and cheer loudly when you run into unexpected troubles." Could that be right? Could James actually be expecting us to paste on a plastic smile when we fall headlong into heartaches? Not at all. James says, *"Consider* it all joy."

In other words, regard it that way. Make a conscious acceptance of the fact. The response he speaks of has more to do with our minds than our emotions.

But why should we regard our problems with joy?

Because we know something, says James. We know that those difficulties—disappointing and distressing as they may be—produce endurance in our lives. Because of those very unwelcome things that have intruded into our personal world, we have the opportunity to develop patience, maturity, and all-around good character.

So why does adversity in my life still surprise me?

There's only one explanation: It's because I keep forgetting what I should know. Sometimes (okay, most of the time) the comfort of not facing difficulty and struggle in my life is a lot more appealing than the character produced by enduring them. When you're comfortable, you don't want to be budged, right? But thankfully, God knows that—in the long run—character is infinitely more important than comfort.

So the trials come. And we get surprised out of our comfortable complacency. Then, later if not sooner, we get around to counting it all joy.

Today—right now—I want to resolve to know something about the intruder that will invariably knock on my door. Before I get up to answer his knock, I want to remember that for all his ill manners, this unwelcome visitor has come for *my good*, for the good of my character. No matter what my emotions tell me, I want to welcome him in. Why? Because down deep, real character is more important to me than temporary comfort.

Will you resolve the same thing with me today? Let's greet that surprise intruder with a surprise of our own.

Joy.

Wayside Interlude

In the multitude of my anxieties within me,
Your comforts delight my soul.

PSALM 94:19, NKJV

The above verse is so amazing. Full of anxieties and perplexities (a "multitude"!), the psalmist experiences something people outside of faith in Jesus Christ could never understand.... Joy. Comfort. Delight. The problems haven't gone away, and the difficulties remain. Yet here is a man who has allowed the Holy Spirit of God to do His encouraging, healing, uplifting work—deep down in his heart of hearts. Have you felt mugged by a gang of anxieties and worries today? Ask God's indwelling Spirit to comfort and strengthen you from the inside out!

PALM WEDNESDAY

They led the donkey and colt out,
laid some of their clothes on them, and Jesus mounted.
Nearly all the people in the crowd threw their garments
down on the road, giving him a royal welcome.
Others cut branches from the trees and threw them down as a
welcome mat. Crowds went ahead and crowds followed,
all of them calling out, "Hosanna to David's son!"
"Blessed is he who comes in God's name!"
"Hosanna in highest heaven!"

MATTHEW 21:7–9, *THE MESSAGE*

Day 13

Shouting their joyful hosannas, the people were caught up in the expectation of Jesus as the coming King. This—at last!—was the one who would throw the Roman oppressor out of the Holy City. He would release them from the terrible burden of taxes. He would feed them, provide for and protect them, and give them national dignity once again.

As the week wore on, however, the mood of the crowd changed.

Why wasn't the Nazarene making His move? Sure, He continued to heal and teach in the temple. But He remained aloof and reclusive, retreating to a nearby village every night, spending time with His disciples outside the city walls. When was He going to *do* something? When was He going to muscle in and take control? Why wasn't He spending time with the "right" people—the savvy political types who got things done?

Little wonder the people's mindset soured by midweek. "Maybe this Man's not all He's cracked up to be," they may have reasoned. "Maybe He's been pulling the wool over our eyes all this time. He's probably powerless to do any real good around here."

The rest is history. The crowds turned on Him and screamed for His crucifixion—not more than a week after they had celebrated His entry into the city.

Sometimes I wonder...are we all that different from those people?

When expectations are running bank high, when we think we've got God's plan neatly figured out, when we've convinced ourselves that the King's job is to make our lives easier, relieve our burdens, and take away our every-day pressures, don't you think our praises may sound a bit empty?

Hosanna! Praise to the King! Hand me a palm branch.

But what happens when the shouts and excitement of Palm Sunday fade into Blue Monday? What happens when we hit midweek and all our anticipation and plans have blown away like smoke in the wind? Can we still sing our hosannas? Or do we turn on God in bitterness or resentment because He didn't "follow through" on our list of expectations?

Let's be sure we give Jesus praise for who He is and what He does.

Not for who we think He ought to be and what we imagine He ought to do.

Wayside Interlude

Even though the fig trees have no blossoms, and there are no grapes on the vine; even though the olive crop fails, and the fields lie empty and barren; even though the flocks die in the fields, and the cattle barns are empty, yet I will rejoice in the LORD! I will be joyful in the God of my salvation.

HABAKKUK 3:17–18, NLT

Please pray with me: *O Lord, am I a fair-weather friend to You? I'm so ready to sing Your praises when my life overflows with blessings. I'm eager to grab the palm branch and shout "Hosanna" when everything has been going my way. But what about those long, weary "Palm Wednesdays"? What's in my heart, what's in my mouth, when life takes a sudden downturn...when sickness sidelines me…when my friends turn cold…when my spouse is too busy to spend time with me and I feel unloved…when others are promoted all around me and I'm left at the back of the pack? Am I as eager to praise You and declare Your worth then? O Lord, so kind and good and wise, may my Hosannas ring out to You every day of my life.*

IF YOU CAN GLORIFY
GOD IN THIS...

*Y*ou hear mothers say it all the time.

Their kids want to stay home, complaining of cramps or a headache. But as soon as the school bus leaves the corner, they bound out of bed, crank up a computer game, turn on the TV, or run downstairs to raid the fridge.

And what do moms all over the world say? "If you're well enough to do *that*, then you're well enough to go to school!"

I heard a similar line while dieting a few months ago. At a friend's house, I turned down a luscious-looking piece of walnut cake topped with whipped cream icing and sprinkled with nuts.

My friend regarded me for a moment. "If you can turn down *this*," she said, "then you can turn down anything."

Maybe you've said something similar as a student, taking way too many units for your own good—and working nights to boot. As the pressure builds, the midnight oil burns, term paper deadlines loom, and finals creep toward you like dark clouds on the horizon, you hear yourself say something like this: "If I can make it through *this* semester, I can make it through anything!"

You can almost hear God say the same thing to us:

...as we absorb crushing disappointments,

...or wrestle with a complicated, confusing family problem,

...or struggle to learn contentment in the midst of a painful illness,

...or tearfully accept the sudden loss of a loved one.

We might at first think it curious that God so often uses suffering to make our lives "to the praise of His glory," as it says in Ephesians 1:12 (NASB). I mean, aren't there better ways we can glorify God? Or at least easier ones?

But do you know what God says to us?

"If you can praise and glorify Me in *this* circumstance, My child, you can glorify Me in anything."

In other words, whenever a Christian is found faithful in affliction, repaying good for evil, returning love for abuse, holding steadfast through suffering, or loving in the middle of loneliness and grief, the Lord receives the truest, brightest, most radiant kind of glory possible. And if we can be found giving Him praise and honor in that manner, God will open up all kinds of new opportunities, new circumstances in which to give Him glory. He'll do so because He knows we can be trusted, we can handle it with His grace.

Maybe today you just can't see glory to God issuing forth from your response to adversity. The laundry is piling up, your friend continues to misunderstand you, you haven't had a restful weekend in who-knows-how-long, and you seem to acquire one miserable sinus infection after another.

Let me tell you something. If you can glorify God

through a patient, trusting response to your troubles right now—if you can!—then you can glorify God anytime, anywhere, in anything.

Wayside Interlude

Rejoice in your hope, be patient in tribulation, be constant in prayer.

ROMANS 12:12, RSV

About midnight Paul and Silas were praying and singing praises to God, while the other prisoners listened. Suddenly a strong earthquake shook the jail to its foundations. The doors opened, and the chains fell from all the prisoners.

ACTS 16:25–26, CEV

Something happens…something supernatural…something powerful…something that touches both time and eternity…when a believer gives praise to Christ in the midst of trouble and adversity. People notice, and wonder. Angels observe, and worship. Demons flee from the brilliance. But more than all of those things, the name of God gains honor and glory. Oh, my friend, it isn't easy. It certainly isn't natural. It may come through tears. But if by faith you will offer a sacrifice of praise to God in the midst of your pain today, the resulting radiance will shine further than you could begin to imagine.

DOES ANYONE
SMELL SMOKE?

*T*he only thing that caught fire were the ropes that bound their hands and feet. Free of their restraints, Shadrach, Meshach, and Abednego seemed to walk about in the great furnace of Babylon like it was an air-conditioned mall on a Sunday afternoon.

And no wonder.

They weren't alone.

Suddenly King Nebuchadnezzar jumped up in alarm and said, "Didn't we throw three men, bound hand and foot, into the fire?"

"That's right, O king," they said.

"But look!" he said. "I see four men, walking around freely in the fire, completely unharmed! And the fourth man looks like a son of the gods!"

DANIEL 3:24–25, *THE MESSAGE*

The king, who had ordered the servants of God thrown into the fire for refusing to worship his golden image, stood as close as he dared to the mouth of the furnace and shouted to them.

"Shadrach, Meshach, and Abednego, servants of the High God, come out here!"

Shadrach, Meshach, and Abednego walked out of the fire.

All the important people, the government leaders and king's counselors, gathered around to examine them and discovered that the fire hadn't so much as touched the three men—not a hair

singed, not a scorch mark on their clothes, not
even the smell of fire on them!

vv. 26–27, *THE MESSAGE*

Not only were the three young men free from burns or
injuries, they didn't even smell like smoke!

At one time or another, all of us have felt the flames of
the Refiner's fire. It's the one experience we all share in
common. No matter how we balk at the idea, God has
promised to refine His children.

To refine, according to *Webster's*, is "to make fine or
pure; free from impurities, dross, alloy, or sediment...to
free from imperfection, coarseness, crudeness, etc." A
refiner, of course, expects to improve whatever commodity
he places into the fire. Look at your gold wedding band,
or maybe that gold chain around your neck. After all these
years, it still gleams. It still wears well. Why? Because it
had the luster and richness pressed into it long ago when
it went through the refining flames.

Look at your best silver, your flatware that you got
when you were married, those silver bowls and trays

tucked away in your china cupboard. You pull them down once in a blue moon, yet they glow with that soft shine even after many years.

The refining process is supposed to turn out things all the more beautiful, all the more durable.

But how many of us go through the Refiner's fire and come out the other end looking like…charcoal? Or rusty iron. Or smoking ashes. We may be like the Pharisees of old who wore long faces and rumpled clothes when they fasted (to attract sympathetic attention). Often when we come through a period of suffering, we want to make sure that everybody knows all the sad and sordid details. The thing of beauty that God wanted to create by sending us into the flames becomes tarnished by our complaints and woebegone expressions.

Be honest. If you've had "one of those days" where you feel like you've been dragged through the Refiner's fire, how do you show it?

❀ By taking a casual greeting like "How are you doing?" as an excuse to list every minor and major casualty of your day?

- By using your prayer group time as an excuse to gripe or gossip?
- By painting a picture of your marriage that colors your spouse as the culprit and you as the hero?
- By living like a martyr...and making sure everybody knows it?

If you do, I'm afraid people are going to smell smoke. They'll know you've been scorched by your troubles, and your testimony may end up tarnished.

There's a better way. Let's offer sincere, wholehearted praise to God as we walk through the Refiner's fire. Perhaps those who pause to peer into our furnace will see the Son of God walking with us.

Day 15

Wayside Interlude

"I'll deliver [them] to the refinery fires.
I'll refine them as silver is refined,
test them for purity as gold is tested.
Then they'll pray to me by name
and I'll answer them personally."

ZECHARIAH 13:9, *THE MESSAGE*

Pray with me: *Father, by the power of Your Holy Spirit within me, I pray that the light and fragrance of Jesus will radiate from my life all day long. No matter what transpires this day, no matter what the weather, no matter what my physical condition, no matter what's transpiring in my family or my most important relationships, I pray that You will enable me to walk in the fire but not smell like smoke. In the name of the One who walks with me, amen.*

GOD CHOOSES THE WEAK

*H*ave you ever thought of the Bible as an adventure story?

The King's most trusted officer turns renegade, gathers a powerful army around him, and leads a rebellion. Through treachery and deceit, the rebel leader usurps the authority of the rightful King, sets up his own rival kingdom, and promptly enslaves its citizens. In order to free the captives and retake the kingdom, the King sends His own Son into the heart of enemy territory...with a battle plan more shocking than anyone could imagine.

It sounds like epic fiction, or the plot for an action-adventure movie. But it's not. The story is as current as this morning's headlines, and the battle blazes white-hot even as you read these words.

Yes, those are real bullets zinging past your head. If anything on this beleaguered planet is real, it is the ceaseless warfare being waged for the hearts and minds of men and women, boys and girls. The stakes in the battle are high, the consequences eternal.

Now…if I were God, seeking to gather a winning team around Jesus Christ, how would I get the job done?

Well, let's see. I'd need a strong economic base. So I'd go after the best brain trust I could pull together. All the Wall Street wizards, Harvard economists, and Fortune 500 guys.

For my strategy team, I'd pursue Nobel Prize laureates, MIT computer analysts, and all the brightest young men and women from the professional world.

For public relations, I'd hire some big Madison Avenue firm. I'd get the best dot-com folks I could find to set up a knockout website. I'd need a front person, of course. Maybe a rugged-looking actor with a deep, smooth voice and a recognizable face. Or a classy blond newswoman, with a face right off a magazine cover, normally found anchoring in primetime on cable TV.

I'd need a tough-minded manager. So why not go for the best? Someone like the president's chief of staff, a retired general, or the CEO of a billion-dollar conglomerate.

With so many educated, blue-chip people—the brightest and the best—the job would surely get done.

But I'm not running the world (aren't you relieved?). God is. And He has already written the most magnificent script imaginable for invading Satan's territory and retaking the Kingdom of Earth under the banner of His Son. But unaccountably…He has peopled the script with the weak and the poor and the unlikely. He casts the roles employing the sick, the lonely, the ungifted, and the unlovely.

Listen to Paul's words…

Notice among yourselves, dear brothers, that few of you who follow Christ have big names or power or wealth. Instead, God has deliberately chosen to

use ideas the world considers foolish and of little
worth in order to shame those people considered
by the world as wise and great. He has chosen a
plan despised by the world, counted as nothing at
all, and used it to bring down to nothing those the
world considers great, so that no one anywhere
can ever brag in the presence of God.

1 CORINTHIANS 1:26–29, TLB

He's chosen such people on His team for a special reason. You see, Satan scoffs at the people God decides on.
He jeers at the insignificant, average, everyday sort of
folks the Lord crowds onto His team. But this is the catch.
If God, by sheer grace, overcomes in spite of the odds,
winning the world by using weak and inferior people,
guess Who receives even greater glory?

Just as it says in 2 Corinthians 12:9: God's power
shows up best in weak people. And if God's power resides
in the weakest of us…if we, through suffering and disappointment, are being groomed for active duty in God's
Special Forces, why should we complain?

Wayside Interlude

He told me, "My grace is enough; it's all you need. My strength comes into its own in your weakness." Once I heard that, I was glad to let it happen. I quit focusing on the handicap and began appreciating the gift. It was a case of Christ's strength moving in on my weakness. Now I take limitations in stride, and with good cheer, these limitations that cut me down to size—abuse, accidents, opposition, bad breaks. I just let Christ take over! And so the weaker I get, the stronger I become.

2 CORINTHIANS 12:9–10, *THE MESSAGE*

Where do you feel especially weak, inadequate, or vulnerable in your life? Invite the Lord to enter into that very area today, and use it for His glory and His kingdom. Then get ready to praise Him for a miracle that will bless other lives and strengthen your faith as never before.

FINGERPRINTS

I remember the time years ago when I had to be fingerprinted by an FBI agent.

No, I'm not confessing here to a life of crime in my past. (Although it might sell a few more books!) Truly, I hadn't done anything wrong at all. I was being fingerprinted because our late, great President Ronald Reagan had nominated me to serve on the National Council on Disability. What an honor that was! But after the nomination the FBI had to do a routine—and exhaustive—investigation on me.

That meant fingerprints.

But there was a problem.

The polite G-man was becoming a little frustrated. Yes, I cooperated to the best of my ability, but have you ever tried fingerprinting a lady who hasn't used her fingers in decades? Silly question. Obviously not. And I didn't think it would be any big deal. But that poor agent had one big headache trying to get prints off the pads of my fingers.

Finally after four or five tries he looked at me, shook his head, and said, "Lady, I'm sorry, but you just don't have any tread on these fingers of yours."

I didn't know what he was talking about until he turned my hand so I could get a good, close look at my own fingers. He was right. I'd never taken the time to examine them before, but the pads of my fingers were super smooth with hardly any ridges at all.

I figured he had run into this sort of thing before, but he said no. The only folks without prints would be people who never used their hands. The agent went on to explain that ridges on fingers deepen with use. The hands of bricklayers, carpenters, data entry folks, and homemakers always have good prints. (I imagine diligent safecrackers would, too!)

Funny. I would have thought just the opposite. It seemed to me that hard work would wear off good fingerprints. But not so. Hard work enhances them.

I think it's the same for people who pour themselves out in service to the Lord. We tend to think Christians who charge full ahead, who give themselves in tireless service, will wear themselves thin. *They'll burn out*, we tell ourselves. *They'll dry up. They'll give themselves to the point of having nothing to give.*

I don't think so. Yes, we need to be wise and leave time in our lives for rest, recreation, and restoration. But I believe that hard work—when accomplished in the power and grace of God—enhances life. Our lives are built up in Christ as we serve Him, not worn down as we might think. Does a fruit tree injure itself by bearing bountiful fruit? Do we question the health of a vine loaded with grapes? Do we worry about an artesian well that keeps bubbling up sweet, clear water hour after hour, day after day?

In his last recorded correspondence, the apostle Paul

wrote to his young friend Timothy that he was being poured out like a drink offering. He had fought the good fight, he had finished the race. But being used up didn't deplete him! His spirit was as strong and great in the Lord Jesus as ever. He had never been more complete, nor life ever as full. And nobody had any trouble tracing his life, identifying his walk with the Lord.

So don't be afraid to give of yourself. If you're tempted to be a shrinking violet in Christ's kingdom, then you will surely shrivel, leaving no prints, no evidence, no means of identifying Jesus to others. No one will be able to trace your walk or follow your steps.

So get in there today and leave fingerprints—good, easy-to-identify fingerprints for God—on everything you do.

If you're ever on trial for being a follower of the Lord Jesus, make sure the prosecution has plenty of evidence.

Wayside Interlude

"He who believes in Me, as the Scripture said, 'From his innermost being shall flow rivers of living water.'"

JOHN 7:38, NASB

Ask God to open your eyes to serve Him today, and throw yourself into that service with all your heart and soul.

Day 18

GOD AND OUR
QUESTIONS

One of the first places I turned after my diving accident was to the book of Job. As I lay immobilized in the hospital, my mind swirled with questions. When I learned that my paralysis was going to be permanent, it raised even more questions.

I was desperate to find answers.

Job, I reasoned, had suffered terribly and questioned God again and again. Perhaps I could find comfort and insight from following his search for answers.

Frankly, it's ironic that many Christians turn to Job for help and comfort. In reality, the book raises more questions than it answers. You'll look in vain through its pages for neat, compact theories on why people suffer. God not only refuses to answer Job's agonized questions, He also declines to comment on all the tidy theological theories offered by Job's erstwhile friends. (Until the end of the book, when He lumps them all together with the phrase, "You have not spoken of me what is right.")

Make no mistake, Job's questions to God weren't of the polite Sunday school variety. They were pointed, sharp, and seemed at times to border on blasphemy.

Why didn't You let me die at birth?

Why didn't You dry up my mother's breasts so that I would starve?

Why do You keep wretched people like me alive?

How do You expect me to have hope and patience?

What do You think I'm made of, anyway? Stone? Metal?

If life is so short, does it have to be miserable, too?

Why don't You back off and quit hurting me for a while?

What did I ever do to You that I became the target for Your arrows?

Why don't You forgive me before I die and it's too late?
How can mortal man be righteous before a holy God?
Why do You favor the wicked?
Since You've already decided I'm guilty, why should I even try?
You're the One who created me, so why are You destroying me?
Why do You hide Your face and consider me Your enemy?
Why don't You let me meet You somewhere face-to-face so I
can state my case?
Why don't You set a time to judge wicked men?

Tough, searching questions. Job didn't toss "softballs" at his God—these queries were sharp and direct. Job's friends were horrified. Scandalized. They half expected lightning to fall and fry the suffering man on the spot.

But the lightning never fell.

And that, to me, is the comfort of the book of Job. What meant most to me in my suffering was that God never condemns Job for his doubt and despair. God was even ready to take on the hard questions. Ah, but the answers? They weren't quite the ones Job was expecting.

Likewise, when it comes right down to it, I'm not sure if it would have sufficed to find "the answers" to all of my questions, anyway. What if God had suddenly consented

to answer all the queries I had sobbed out to Him in the
middle of the night? Could I have even begun to handle
those answers? It would have been like dumping a water
tower into a teacup. Pouring Lake Erie into a thimble. My
poor pea brain wouldn't have been able to process it.

For some reason, however, it comforted me to realize
that God did not condemn me for plying Him with questions. I didn't have to worry about insulting God by my
outbursts in times of stress and fear and pain. My despair
wasn't going to shock Him. God, according to the book of
Job, is never threatened by our questions.

And so…did I find answers? Answers to the deepest,
darkest questions about a life of total paralysis?

Just one. But it is enough. I think I'll let Paul put it in
his own words.

Have you ever come on anything quite like this
extravagant generosity of God, this deep, deep
wisdom? It's way over our heads. We'll never fig-
ure it out. "Is there anyone around who can
explain God? Anyone smart enough to tell him
what to do? Anyone who has done him such a

huge favor that God has to ask his advice?"
Everything comes from him; everything happens
through him; everything ends up in him. Always
glory! Always praise! Yes. Yes. Yes.

ROMANS 11:33–36, *THE MESSAGE*

Wayside Interlude

"I am nothing—how could I ever find the
answers? I will put my hand over my mouth in
silence. I have said too much already. I have nothing more to say."

JOB 40:4–5, NLT

*Thank You, Father, for hearing my heart-cry on dark nights
and gray days when my soul was wrapped in pain and fear and
sorrow. Thank You for not condemning me, or turning away from
me, or shaming me. When I have cried out and thrown questions at
You from the deep well of my suffering, You chose to bear with me,
to draw close to me, and to bring comfort into my life in a thousand*

ways. I may always have questions, Father, but I'm learning that the answer beyond all answers is to simply cling to You. In the name of Your Son who has given me confident access to Your awesome presence, amen.

Day 19

BY LOVE CONSTRAINED

A number of years ago I flew into Indiana for a speaking engagement at a church. One of the pastors met me at the airport, escorted me to his car, and whisked me across the lush, summer countryside.

As we discussed his church, I often glanced out the window at the beautiful fields passing by. I commented on what a lovely area it was. Great farmland. Rich acres of corn and all sorts of vegetables. It was a treat to the eye; the countryside seemed especially productive.

"Wasn't always like this," my driver replied with a smile.

"Really?" I asked. "What do you mean?"

"At one time this whole area was marshland. One big swamp."

The pastor had my complete attention as he went on to describe how a nearby river would overflow its low banks every spring, rendering all of that prime land useless. To counter that annual dilemma, the state undertook a vast engineering project to build up the river banks through that vulnerable area. as a result, the waters of the river were controlled and channeled, freeing up rich acres of productive farmland.

He compared what happened there to the love of God in our lives. He mentioned Paul's words in 2 Corinthians 5:14: "For the love of Christ constraineth us" (KJV).

"I'm glad you brought that up," I told him, "because I've never really known what 'constraineth' actually means."

He laughed. "Well, Joni, as I understand it, constraining means to *press in*…in order to *push forward*. When that river was pressed in on each side by reinforced banks, the

flow of water was constrained, or pushed forward, resulting in more productive farmland.

"It's the same with us," he went on. "Sometimes God
in His love brings about circumstances which seem to
press in on every side — walled situations or high hedges
where we feel closed in. Yet God allows these crushing
pressures to ultimately push us forward and make us more
effective, more productive. Though we may not like it, the
trials press us and push us in a better direction — a direction God wants us to head."

Though the years have rolled by, I have never forgotten that word picture from that Indiana pastor. The Lord
brings it back to my mind on those occasions when the
walls of my world seem to be closing in on me.

Is it like that for you today? Do you feel barricaded
and pushed upon from every side? Could it be that God is
beginning to press you in…for the purpose of compelling
you forward? Could it be that those hardships you're
experiencing are evidences of the constraining love of
Christ?

It may be that your life hasn't been as fruitful or productive as you know it might have been. Wandering

without direction, you sense wasted time, wasted energy. Instead of a rich field of grain, your life seems more like a stagnant swamp.

Thank God for His sovereign intrusion into your life. Thank Him that He loves you too much to let you wander, wasting your life and energies. He's involved in a profound engineering project in your life, and your circumstances—even the pushing, squeezing, distressing ones—are part of that plan. Though it may not feel like it right now, it's a plan to make your life more productive than you ever dreamed possible.

That's divine engineering at its best.

Wayside Interlude

I think you ought to know, dear brothers and sisters, about the trouble we went through in the province of Asia. We were crushed and completely overwhelmed, and we thought we would never live through it. In fact, we expected to die. But as a result, we learned not to rely on ourselves, but on God who can raise the dead. And he did deliver us…And we are confident that he will continue to deliver us.

2 CORINTHIANS 1:8–10, NLT

Reflect on those circumstances in your life today that constrain you, limit you, or press in on you. By faith, thank the Father that these very things —distressing or frustrating as they might be — will teach you more about His character, His power to deliver, and His overcoming love. In the process, your life will become more fruitful and productive for Him.

Day 20

GRACE ON DISPLAY

The jade was exquisite. Smooth, glossy, and finely carved. Delicate gold chains cradled the light and returned it, ripe and mellow. Translucent opals graced their settings with milky fire.

Yes, I confess. I've been window-shopping in the mall. I was only going to linger at the jewelry store a moment, but the artistry of those precious stones held me a bit longer than I'd intended.

The diamonds, set against a black yard of velvet, were radiant—breaking the light into flashes of color. It seemed as though the contrast between the black velvet and the diamonds made those gems all the more brilliant. No other color cloth would have done—no blues, no grays, no pinks.

Midnight velvet produced the best contrast.

No, I didn't buy a diamond that day. But as I wheeled back through the parking lot to my van, I kept thinking about that jeweler's display. It struck me as just one more illustration of how God works in our lives.

I thought about contrasts. A black night seems to make the moon brighter. Purple irises brighten yellow daffodils. And a dark gray Kansas sky makes the wheat look truly golden.

So it is with us. It seems that God best displays the brilliance of His grace against the backdrop of our dark and even blackest moments. Somehow, His grace is made all the more glorious when people see it at work in the lives of those who suffer.

Paul expressed a thought like that in a letter to the church in Corinth:

For God, who said, "Let there be light in the darkness," has made us understand that this light is the
brightness of the glory of God that is seen in the
face of Jesus Christ.

But this precious treasure—this light and
power that now shine within us—is held in per-
ishable containers, that is, in our weak bodies.
So everyone can see that our glorious power is
from God and is not our own.

2 CORINTHIANS 4:6-7, NLT

I don't know how often you're prone to stopping by
display cases in jewelry stores. And I'm not sure if you've
ever thought about why they display those precious stones
the way they do. But as you read these words, you may
feel as though your life is blanketed by blackness. Maybe
you don't see much rhyme or reason behind that dark cur-
tain of discouragement or grief right now. As difficult as
this thought may be to understand, God wants to use your
life as a display case for a while. He wants your life to be a
setting where He can display His grace for all to see.

The contrast between your suffering and God's grace

is going to catch the attention of people wandering through the mall of life. They'll be drawn to God's display case. Your life will be set apart from the rest of the ordinary stones and settings around you. Believers and unbelievers alike will be drawn to you.

Why? To observe the black backdrop? Of course not. They will be attracted by the extraordinary beauty and radiance of God's grace in your life.

You will discover that God's power shows up best against your weakness.

Wayside Interlude

We are pressed on every side by troubles, but we are not crushed and broken. We are perplexed, but we don't give up and quit. We are hunted down, but God never abandons us. We get knocked down, but we get up again and keep going. Through suffering, these bodies of ours constantly share in the death of Jesus so that the life of Jesus may also be seen in our bodies.

2 CORINTHIANS 4:8–10, NLT

Since the bright, beautiful presence of Jesus has actually taken up residence inside our lives, we are containers of glory! And what happens if there is a crack or break in that container? Light blazes out through the opening! Beauty rushes out through our wounds, brokenness, and imperfections. What a God we have! Praise Him today for His plan to display His grace in and through our lives —and especially in our weakness.

EVERY GOOD GIFT

$\mathcal{H}$ave you ever sat down at your computer, opened a file, and started listing all the good things that God has brought into your life? Maybe you've gotten as far as twenty items and thought you were done. After all, you had to stretch your thinking to be even *that* specific.

Ah, but there's more. So much more than we can possibly imagine. If we let the full impact of a verse like James 1:17 blow apart our ideas about God's blessings, we'd see our list suddenly stretch past the horizon.

Listen to this familiar verse in *The Message* paraphrase:

Every desirable and beneficial gift comes out of
heaven. The gifts are rivers of light cascading
down from the Father of Light.

Rivers of light! Every good gift falling from heaven!
Think of it. James is saying that every good time you've
ever had in this world comes directly from God. (I mean
good times — not sinful times.)

Can you think of the times you ever laughed and
enjoyed yourself on an evening with friends? Can you
remember the funny jokes? Can you recall the first time
you won a game of Monopoly — flush with fake cash but
feeling like a miniature tycoon? Can you remember your
first date? Well, maybe you'd like to *forget* the first date.
How about your fifth date, when things got a little more
comfortable? How about your first crack at water or snow
skiing?

Or a special walk with a little child who loved you?

Or that special evening with your family by a campfire, under the star-strewn heavens?

Can you remember hearing some music that went right to your heart and brought goose bumps to your back or tears to your eyes? The Bible says here that your Father is the origin of every joyful smile that has ever crossed your face.

How about God's provision of good food? Summer-fresh corn on the cob with lots of butter and salt and pepper. Rich, moist, double-layer chocolate cake. Or maybe a juicy hamburger with all the trimmings! When you think about it, God could have made all our nourishment taste the same. But no, instead He chose to make our food taste good, and created our taste buds to appreciate every bite. He even created brussels sprouts to…well, I'm not sure why He created brussels sprouts.

And then there is color. People as old as me might remember the Disney TV theme from years ago: *"The world is a carousel of color…."* And so it is. When you think about it, the Creator didn't have to make a world in color. He could have wrapped it all in battleship gray. Think of all the beautiful sunsets—one every minute all over the world, like a rolling wave of radiance. Picture the spongy green of spring-fresh grass or the pink of a hyacinth or crocus. In a recent news item about a middle-aged man who gained his sight after a lifetime of blindness, the awestruck man was quoted as saying, "I never imagined that yellow could be so...*yellow.*"

Our God is the God of sunrise splendor, the haunting loveliness of the northern lights, the explosion of color from the heart of a diamond, and, well, so many wonderful things I couldn't list them in a million pages. Things like...

...hot buttered popcorn,

...red rosebuds, wet with dew,

...spring rain,

...Thanksgiving turkey,

...bear hugs from your best friend,

...freshly laundered towels,

...ice tea on a hot summer day,

...the cheery warmth of a winter fire,

...and the laughter of a child.

Every good thing comes from the Father. "Every desirable and beneficial gift." Every single one. And more than that, these good things are *gifts*. Gifts to be received with heartfelt gratitude. As David wrote, "How precious to me are your thoughts, O God! How vast is the sum of them! Were I to count them, they would outnumber the grains of sand" (Psalm 139:17–18).

All too often, though, you and I save our mental checklists for all the bad and discouraging things — especially when we're facing times of adversity. We file away in our thinking all the times we've ever been disappointed, embarrassed, used, humiliated, or hurt. And soon we find ourselves irritated and complaining — clutched at the throat by an ungrateful spirit.

Even though our own pain might scream for our individual attention, God wants us to come to Him with a heart full of thankfulness for all the good things in life. Everything from the joy of a Christ-centered friendship to the first lick of a double-scoop pistachio-almond-fudge ice cream cone.

Every good gift comes from the same Giver.

Wayside Interlude

Unfailing love and truth have met together.
  Righteousness and peace have kissed!

Truth springs up from the earth,
  and righteousness smiles down from heaven.

Yes, the LORD pours down his blessings.
  Our land will yield its bountiful crops.

Righteousness goes as a herald before him,
  preparing the way for his steps.

PSALM 85:10–13, NLT

What are some of the good gifts that you have experienced in the last few days? Think carefully. Remember some really wonderful gifts come from the hand of God disguised as something else! Offer your thanksgiving today to the Father of Light.

OUR ADVERSITY... AND A WATCHING WORLD

I blew the dust off an old quote the other day. It was in one of those obscure volumes off the top shelf in a back closet—one that would have never made it into a stack of bestsellers at Wal-Mart or Costco.

The phrase went like this: *"The final crown of glory in this world is martyrdom, and the blood of the martyrs is the seed of the church."*

Don't hear that kind of talk much these days, do we?

It's not the kind of feel-good stuff that draws top ratings on Christian talk shows. That's one quote you'll never see stitched in needlepoint in the family room, or inscribed in gold calligraphy on a greeting card. Not the sort of phrase likely to end up on a T-shirt or followed by a smiley face at the end of an e-mail.

Words like those seem a little musty…linked to another age, long ago and far away.

That may be true in our comfortable Western world. But in many parts of the world today, that statement on martyrdom is as current as the morning newspaper. Every day believers in Christ are being persecuted, hounded from one place to another, subjected to humiliation and torture, or killed for the simple reason that they own the name of Jesus.

And it's still true to this moment: *Nothing, nothing, nothing draws the attention of unbelievers like the way believers endure hardship.* What, they ask themselves, is the mysterious power that enables these people to remain so calm—even joyful—in the middle of terrible circumstances?

Most of our trials are Styrofoam-light compared to

what the martyrs of the church endured—and still endure. As Scripture reminds us, most of us have never suffered to the point of shedding blood in our struggle against sin (Hebrews 12:4). No lions, no fiery death at the stake, no facing a firing squad.

When we do suffer—whether from the bumps and bruises of daily living or for our testimony for Jesus—we ought to respond with double the thanksgiving and triple the joy.

The Lord has spared contemporary believers in the Western world from so much pain and suffering. He has been so gracious to us! Perhaps even to the point that when trials do come our way we are "surprised…as though something strange were happening" to us (1 Peter 4:12).

But it's as true now as it was hundreds of years ago. Nothing will confound, convict, and convince those around us like the peaceful and positive way you and I respond to our twenty-first-century hurts and distress. The unbelieving world—your neighbors, the guy at the gas station, the postman, the lady at the cleaners, your boss at work—observes the way we undergo our trials.

By God's grace, you can hang on without a grumble or complaint, remain joyful in tribulation, shun the temptation to grandstand as a "martyr," offer thanks in all things, and trust and obey no matter what.

It may not be martyrdom, but it will still startle and puzzle a watching world. It will still compel seeking men and women to reconsider Jesus.

Wayside Interlude

You need neither fear men's threats nor worry about them; simply concentrate on being completely devoted to Christ in your hearts. Be ready at any time to give a quiet and reverent answer to any man who wants a reason for the hope that you have within you.

1 PETER 3:15, PHILLIPS

What would make someone ask about the hope in our lives? Perhaps it is the contrast that catches their attention—everyone else is complaining and griping, but you're not; everyone else is nervous and uptight, but you have a peace that radiates from within; everyone else is pushing for more money, more prestige, more toys, and more entertainment, but you have a quiet contentment about your life. The simple keys are in the verse above: Concentrate on being devoted to Christ, and be ready at all times to explain the reason for the hope and joy that they can't miss!

WHAT ARE the "ALL THINGS"?

And we know that in all things
God works for the good of those who love him.

ROMANS 8:28

Y ou've seen it inscribed on little magnets on
refrigerator doors. It shows up now and then on
key rings. And I've even noticed it hand embroidered
on a teddy bear. You've probably memorized it in a couple

of different translations…and maybe had it quoted to you on occasions when you didn't want to hear it.

Could it be that we take Romans 8:28 for granted because it's so familiar?

I happened to be looking at the verse the other day when a question I'd never considered popped into my mind. I found myself wondering, What did the apostle Paul have in mind when he wrote that all things work together for good? More specifically, what did he mean by "all"? What things could he have been thinking about?

As I read on from that passage, I came across some surprising answers to those queries. Toward the end of the chapter, Paul begins to define what kinds of "things" he's talking about.

To put it in a nutshell, the list isn't very pretty. It's not the kind of stuff you'd cross-stitch for your wall or embroider on a teddy bear's tummy.

He starts with the word *trouble*, and moves on from there to *hardship*. After these, he pencils in *persecution, famine, nakedness, danger,* and *the sword*.

Quite a list. And these are the things he believed God fit together for good in his life! He endured, confident that

no amount of trouble or hardship—in whatever form—
could separate him from the love of God.

Somehow, I can't picture Paul looking at the words of
Romans 8:28 with a "ho-hum-I've-heard-it-all-before" attitude. I can't conceive of him being casual or nonchalant
about such wonderful truth. I get the distinct impression
that items like nakedness, danger, and the sword kept him
on his toes, kept him close to God.

What are the "all things" in your life today? What list
could you come up with? Now, thank God, famine might
not lead your list. I'm guessing that nakedness or the
sword might not crop up, either. Your list might not even
include persecution.

Even so, you still have a list. And it's as heartfelt to
you as Paul's was to him. Can you thank God for working
all the circumstances and events of your life together for
good? Can you grasp the fact that today's list of troubles
can never, ever separate you from the love of God? Nor
tomorrow's?

Don't let Romans 8:28 become like an old, worn pair
of slippers. Don't shuffle through life with it. Don't let
the truth of God's sovereign dealings in the lives of His

children become some detached, abstract fact of life.
Every time you encounter a new setback, struggle, or
obstacle in your life, Romans 8:28 can bloom with new
meaning, new encouragement, new hope.

It's as new as tomorrow's sunrise, and as fresh as your
next hardship.

Wayside Interlude

Before I was afflicted I went astray,
but now I obey your word....
It was good for me to be afflicted
so that I might learn your decrees.

PSALM 119:67, 71

*It is understandably easy to pick and choose which things in
our lives to give thanks for. It's as though the adverse, trying circumstances that enter our lives somehow slipped past God's filter
simply to plague us. But the Bible tells a different story. Think
through the difficulties you've faced in the past week. How can you
offer God praise today—and brag on His name a little to others—
for the very things that distressed you or put you in a bind?*

NO DIFFERENT STORY

The writer of Hebrews describes Scripture as a sharp sword. From my perspective, it often feels more like a needle.

One verse that has needled me for years is 1 Corinthians 10:13:

> No temptation has seized you except what is common to man. And God is faithful; he will not let you be tempted beyond what you can bear. But

when you are tempted, he will also provide a way
out so that you can stand up under it.

Why does that verse prick me so? Because every now
and then I'm tempted to think that God *couldn't* expect
from me what He does from others. Obviously, it's a different story in my case, right?

I remember lying on my hospital bed as a scared
teenager, thinking that God was putting me through more
than I could take. *Paralysis. Total and permanent.* But there
was 1 Corinthians 10:13, reminding me that God is faithful, and that He will not let me be tempted beyond what I
can bear.

The verse came back to pierce me again when I was in
my late twenties, single, and with every prospect of
remaining so. Sometimes lust or a bit of fantasizing would
seem so inviting—and so easy to justify. After all, hadn't I
already given up more than most Christians just by being
disabled? Didn't my wheelchair entitle me to a little slack
now and then? Maybe some special consideration?

Yet there were those words, staring up at me from the
pages of my Bible. *God is faithful...He will not let you be*

tempted beyond what you can bear…He will provide a way
out…you can stand up under it.

When God allows you to suffer, do you have the tendency to use your very trials as an excuse for sinning? Or do you feel that since you've given God a little extra lately by taking such abuse, He owes you a free pass or a day off?

I have a hunch we've all experienced this inner battle. But when we sit down and examine our lame protests in the strong light of a verse like 1 Corinthians 10:13, the excuses just fade away, one by one.

The truth of the matter is, when we sin during our sufferings, it's not because ours is a "different story" and we're forced to disobey. We don't sin because we have to. We sin because we *want* to.

God gives me grace to live in a wheelchair that He doesn't give you if you can walk. But He gives you the grace to endure an unwanted divorce or the death of a spouse or the loss of a job or the rebellion of a child, which He doesn't give to me. God provides the way of escape, the means by which we may bear up under our individual trials.

The question is never, "Can you obey?"
It's more like, "*Will* you obey?"

Wayside Interlude

He will keep you strong right up to the end, and
he will keep you free from all blame on the great
day when our Lord Jesus Christ returns. God will
surely do this for you, for he always does just what
he says, and he is the one who invited you into this
wonderful friendship with his Son, Jesus Christ
our Lord.

1 Corinthians 1:8–9, nlt

*In the potent little book of Zephaniah, God declares to Israel,
"I care about sin with a fiery passion" (1:18, The Message).
Have you allowed yourself to imagine that God will overlook or
wink at your "little sins" because of what you have suffered or
endured? It's not true! All sin is a great offense to God. Ask His
indwelling Holy Spirit to search your heart, and reveal those atti-
tudes, thoughts, words, and actions that cause Him grief.*

THE EXCHANGE

I'm intrigued by the crosses people wear around their necks.

My niece has a delicate little cross of pearls and gold. An Episcopalian friend of mine has one of those big chunky crosses made of brass. My brother-in-law favors a silver cross, with turquoise bits on it, hanging from a leather necklace.

What fascinates me most is the idea of wearing a cross at all.

Why would we?

After all, a cross is an instrument of torture. An execution machine. Some might say it would be the same as wearing a little silver guillotine, a gilded hangman's noose, or an electric chair made of tiny pearls.

Sounds strange, doesn't it? What makes a cross different from other devices of torture? I once heard Elisabeth Elliot say that Christians have exchanged its meaning for something entirely new and wonderful. To us, the very contrivance which killed our Lord Jesus has become the trademark of our hope and salvation. What was once a symbol of horrible death miraculously becomes a symbol of eternal life.

Maybe that's what happened with this wheelchair of mine. To many, it's something which symbolizes confinement, alienation, illness, weakness, and suffering. But because of the grace of God in my life, its meaning has been exchanged for something new and, yes, wonderful. This paralysis of mine has drawn me so much closer to Christ. It has given me a richer experience of His grace, encouragement, and sustaining power.

Perhaps something similar has happened in your experience with Christ as well. Your symbol may be a back brace instead of a wheelchair. A cane, a hearing aid, or a pair of thick glasses. Or perhaps a birthmark, a prominent scar, or a disfigurement of some sort. Maybe an event or a series of circumstances. Perhaps even a disabled child.

Suffering in itself, of course, is a distressing, negative experience. Who likes it? Who wants it? Even so, when Christ exchanged the meaning of the cross for something new, He was able to open up a whole realm of possibilities in our suffering. Through the victory of the cross, He enables us to gain victory in our suffering. So much so that we, too, can ascribe radiant new meaning to otherwise hurtful and sorrowful circumstances.

I don't need to go so far as to wear a little turquoise wheelchair around my neck. But the principle is still the same. My disability…your heartaches and hardships…can take on new meaning through Christ.

Wayside Interlude

As for me, God forbid that I should boast about anything except the cross of our Lord Jesus

Christ. Because of that cross, my interest in this world died long ago, and the world's interest in me is also long dead.

GALATIANS 6:14, NLT

Only God can turn our most devastating trials into trophies of His grace. Only the sovereign Lord can take our darkest days and use them to bring us to pathways of brightest light and joy and kingdom service. Read Psalm 40:1–3, then tell someone how the Lord lifted you from a pit, placed your feet on solid ground, and put a new song in your mouth.

Day 26

SELF-PITY AT THE DOOR

*T*he modern technology which has brought us so many helpful new products, plastics, insecticides, and preservatives looms like a deadly curse for a friend of mine.

Linda has been chemically poisoned. As a result, she's lost the ability to tolerate this synthetic world of ours. I went to see her last week at her little place tucked back in the Santa Barbara hills. For two weeks prior, I had to go through a total "detoxification" of my clothes, my body, and my hair. I couldn't use any perfumes, deodorants, or soaps. I couldn't even eat garlic or onion or anything spicy.

As we ate together in her home, Linda described an incident from the previous week. She had been forced to endure a lengthy confinement in her bedroom simply because the neighbors down the road were having a bar-beque. One whiff of wind-blown lighter fluid can cause her to lose consciousness.

Because of her disability, Linda is mostly alone, isolated from friends and family. Yet her solitude is often disturbed by a persistent visitor at her door. This unwelcome acquaintance knocks and knocks, whining and pleading to get in.

His name is self-pity.

It's certainly easy to understand why Linda feels tempted to let this unrelenting visitor in. It would be easy to feel sorry for herself when she has to use some ancient, metal piece of phone equipment with deteriorating parts that can't be replaced. Her shouted conversations over that technology dinosaur leave her frustrated, exhausted—and more isolated than ever.

Does she have it rough? Uh-huh.

Don't you think she deserves some time for a few hours' visit with self-pity? Some people would say yes, and understandably so.

But Linda? Listen to what she told me.

"No, Joni, suffering and sickness and pain don't rank high on my list of best possible options for a happy life. But God alone can determine what's best for me. Only He sees the beginning from the end. He's the only One who knows what it will take to conform me to the image of His Son. And He spares no pain in accomplishing His will in my life. I don't need pity. And what I need even less is my own pity."

We all find days when self-pity, like an unrelenting stalker, keeps peering in our windows or trying to slip in through the back door. These are days when we feel like nobody understands how tough we have it, what we've been through, or what we have to deal with.

Ah, poor me! you think to yourself.

Before you offer hospitality to self-pity—before you let him settle in and kick off his shoes—remember a lady named Linda in a little house in the Santa Barbara hills. Linda…who endures so much aloneness, but surrounds herself with the prayers of caring Christian friends, and refuses to allow self-pity to even get a foot in the door.

If she can keep that door closed and latched, so can you.

Wayside Interlude

Actually, I don't have a sense of needing anything personally. I've learned by now to be quite content whatever my circumstances. I'm just as happy with little as with much, with much as with little. I've found the recipe for being happy whether full or hungry, hands full or hands empty. Whatever I have, wherever I am, I can make it through anything in the One who makes me who I am.

PHILIPPIANS 4:11–13, *THE MESSAGE*

Day 26

The best way to keep self-pity from gaining a foothold in the living room of our souls is to refuse her entrance altogether. Ignore her knocks on the door. Close your ears to her sad and sorrowful voice on your front steps. Denied entrance, she will go away. Encouraged even in the smallest ways, she will move in and become a permanent resident.

HIGH-STAKES ATTITUDES

*L*et's talk about a few facts of life.

Tires have blowouts, computer hard drives crash, toddlers get colds, and picnics invite rain. If that isn't enough, somebody gets a promotion ahead of us, a babysitting arrangement falls through, a long-planned vacation gets canceled at the last minute, we don't make the team at school, or the heartthrob we're interested in dating is "busy" on four consecutive weekends.

Some things simply can't be avoided.

Now, we aren't always responsible for the circumstances in which we find ourselves. When things happen they just happen, and many times there is little we can do about it.

But before we think we're totally absolved from any responsibility in a difficult circumstance, let's look at one additional fact of life. We *are* responsible for the way we respond to those everyday setbacks. We can either choose to indulge ourselves in depression, backbiting, or bitterness...or we can choose to look to our sovereign God who has everything under our control and holds "our times" in His hand (Psalm 31:14–15).

You see, we are not without choices!

I'm impressed with the way the apostle Paul assumed responsibility over his attitude toward the disappointments and hard blows of life. In the midst of an undeserved prison sentence and in the face of an uncertain future, he went on record saying, "I want to report to you, friends, that my imprisonment here has had the opposite of its intended effect. Instead of being squelched, the Message has actually prospered" (Philippians 1:12, *The Message*).

Paul must have realized that he had very little control over the sometimes devastating circumstances of his life. He couldn't have avoided the shipwreck. He had no control over the phony apostles who were jealous of him and tried to slander his reputation. He never asked to be dropped unceremoniously over the city wall in a basket. Nor did he enlist the service of a demon-possessed girl to follow him around Philippi, shouting at the top of her lungs. And when he answered people's direct questions, could he help it if the truth made them angry?

Yet Paul realized that his reaction—how he responded before many watching eyes—to negative circumstances was serious business. His reactions could either advance Christ's kingdom or set it back. In other words, *there was much more at stake than simply Paul's life.* Other lives would be influenced by his calm, faith-filled response to the adversity, injustice, and pain he experienced. The reputation of Christ's message was at stake. Angels were watching. God was taking notice.

What then, about me? I'm not in prison as Paul was. No guard stands outside my bedroom door. No chains dangle from my wrists, and no manacles bite into my ankles.

But I do have a wheelchair. And as with Paul, I can't claim direct responsibility for this particular circumstance.

But please hear me. *I am responsible.* I am responsible in a deep, profound way, with implications reaching into eternity. I will be held accountable for my response to these "chains." In company with Paul the apostle, I'm learning to embrace joy by faith, because my paralysis — much like those chains — is being used to advance God's cause. Of that I have no doubt, and because of that, I can find reason to be thankful.

No, you may not be responsible for that irritating phone call from your neighbor, or for the fact that your husband will be late getting home from work, or that your wife can't seem to balance the checkbook. But you are responsible for how you respond to those things, and you will be held accountable by the living God for the choices you make.

If you keep a good attitude in the tough times today, it will, in effect, turn out for the advantage of the gospel. As others see, as your husband takes notice, as your children observe, as your neighbors look on, as you speak out with boldness and humility—you will advance God's cause.

There's so much more at stake here than simply your own life. Others can be influenced to make eternal decisions. The good news of Jesus Christ has a reputation, and angels are observing.

So is God.

Wayside Interlude

Therefore, since we are surrounded by such a huge crowd of witnesses to the life of faith, let us strip off every weight that slows us down, especially the sin that so easily hinders our progress. And let us run with endurance the race that God has set before us. We do this by keeping our eyes on Jesus, on whom our faith depends from start to finish.

HEBREWS 12:1–2, NLT

Who are these "witnesses," this huge crowd which watches our life of faith from the grandstand? Could this mean angelic hosts, the Bible heroes of old, or even our own loved ones and believing ancestors who have gone on into eternity before us? We may never know on this side of heaven. But we probably do know many of those who watch us carefully—without our even knowing it. Our spouse. Our kids. Our neighbors. Our coworkers. The lady at the espresso hut and the man who fills our gas tank. How WE run our race, cling to our faith, and fix our eyes on Jesus may change THEIR lives forever.

Day 28

THE OTHER KIND OF SUFFERING

Her name is Kerrie. She's the thirteen-year-old daughter of one of the women I work with in the office. Kerrie occasionally volunteers after school at her mother's side, stuffing envelopes, photocopying resource lists, and sorting brochures. She's a shy little girl who spends a lot of time alone, reading, drawing, and doing puzzles.

There's a deeper reason why Kerrie is so shy, so withdrawn.

Middle school hasn't been easy for her. She's the one who's left out in the cafeteria. She's the one who walks down the hall alone. She's the target of the name-callers. She's the one who's had to brush dried food out of her hair—food thrown by hateful classmates.

I look at her and am bewildered. I simply don't understand.

Kerrie is a kind, sensitive girl with a smattering of pale freckles across cheeks that apple-up when she smiles. She offers no retort to her tormentors, no resistance, no angry backbiting. I haven't figured out why the boys and girls in her school treat her so spitefully. What makes it so cruel is the anguish this girl suffers. Deep pain and perplexity, smothered and suppressed, still show in her eyes.

Does our Lord identify with *that* kind of suffering?

We all know how Jesus suffered. Maybe we can visualize scenes from Mel Gibson's movie *The Passion of the Christ*. We picture the crown of thorns the soldier ground down into His scalp, or the nails driven through His hands and feet. The cross, understandably, is synonymous with the suffering of Christ.

But sometimes it's hard to identify with that kind of

pain. Yes, He suffered unbearably during those dark
hours, but that's not the sort of suffering most of us have
to face. As with my young friend Kerrie, our suffering is
often on the *inside*. Out of sight. Bloodless. Silent. Hidden
from others.

We often suffer intense relational pain—the hurts,
slights, rejections, and put-downs inflicted by others.
No, it isn't a scourging or a beating. There aren't any lit-
eral nails or thorns. But it still hurts. Sometimes
unbearably so.

Can we be certain our Lord identifies with that sort of
nonspectacular, "everyday" pain?

Isaiah 53 lays any such doubt to rest. In verse after
verse the prophet paints a profoundly personal portrait of
the Messiah. Within those lines—and often between the
lines—we catch a glimpse of the everyday pain Jesus
Christ endured as He walked on the earth.

Early in the chapter we learn that Jesus was not nec-
essarily the most attractive guy on earth. Isaiah writes:
"There was nothing beautiful or majestic about his appearance, nothing to attract us to him. He was despised and

rejected—a man of sorrows, acquainted with bitterest grief" (Isaiah 53:2–3, NLT).

There was nothing about His physical appearance that particularly drew people. He was just an everyday, ordinary-looking, Jewish young man.

There are plenty of plain Jane and John Does who can identify with Isaiah 53:2. I've had those days, too—days when you look in the mirror and feel downright unattractive. Maybe even ugly. But the Bible tells us that we have a Savior who knows what that sort of rejection and loneliness is all about.

Verse 6 reveals even more: "All of us have strayed away like sheep. We have left God's paths to follow our own. Yet the LORD laid on him the guilt and sins of us all" (NLT).

Everybody turned away from Him. Alone, Jesus shouldered the burden of our sin and rebellion.

We turned our backs on him and looked the other way when he went by. He was despised, and we did not care.

v. 3, NLT

Just as you have felt the stab of other people's pity or the indifference of uncaring friends, Jesus, too, endured the sting of rebuff and the ache of loneliness. And it wasn't an occasional thing from a few fair-weather friends. He felt the awful realization that *no one* was on His side. No one bothered to listen or care.

Verse 11 speaks of the "suffering of his soul." That has to be the worst kind of suffering possible...when you cry those deep, heaving sobs that come from way down inside. Real anguish you just can't stop.

You know how that feels. So does He.

So if you're experiencing relational pain today, battling that ache that goes right through you, remember that Jesus, your High Priest, perfectly understands.

Yes, His suffering went far beyond what you and I will ever understand—all the way to the cross. But He also understands how it feels to be ignored, spurned, and devalued.

If you bring that pain to Him, He will never make light of it.

Wayside Interlude

When they hurled their insults at him, he did not
retaliate; when he suffered, he made no threats.
Instead, he entrusted himself to him who judges
justly.

1 PETER 2:23

*Because Jesus physically walked on our world and shared the
experience of human life with us, we can be sure He understands
ALL of our pain. "I honor my Father and you dishonor me," He
told a gathering of His countrymen (John 8:49). Bring it all to
Him today—all the slights, unfair criticisms, cutting remarks,
and hurtful treatment. He understands. He has taken note of
everything. And He knows how to bring healing to the deepest, most
hidden parts of your soul.*

LIFELINE

hose early days when I first got out of the hospital were terrifying. Without the encouragement and perspective of Scripture, I honestly don't know how I would have survived. Like a strong lifeline, God's Word kept me from drowning in my despair.

Several of those lifeline passages were from a single chapter in the book of Lamentations. In one verse, Jeremiah wrote: "The LORD is good to those who wait for

Him, to the soul who seeks Him" (Lamentations 3:25,
NKJV).

What else did I have to do but wait? The long, lonely
hours in the middle of the night were bearable because of
that promise. God would be good. To me. I was waiting,
and I would see His goodness. The prophet goes on to say,
"It is good that one should hope and wait quietly for the
salvation of the LORD" (v. 26, NKJV).

Salvation.

Deliverance.

It was a promise, right there in black and white. And
though I had no use of my hands, I clung to that lifeline
with all the hope that was in me. I waited and believed
that deliverance (whatever that meant) would surely
come. In the next verse, Jeremiah says:

It is good for a man to bear the yoke in his youth.
Let him sit alone and keep silent, because God has
laid it on him.

3 : 2 7 – 2 8 , N K J V

Some things are harder to learn as we get older. Our hearts may be calloused or indifferent. Perhaps age brings about the feeling of being worldly wise. We've "seen it all," and there is nothing new to learn. For all the pain of shattered dreams, a yoke is better borne in youth.

As a young teenager, my heart was still at a tender age. I was still hammering out values and principles. There was still much to learn; in my deepest heart I knew that was true. So I stepped into the great unknown and, by sheer faith, trusted that it was good to bear such a heavy yoke of disability in my youth.

But the best part of Lamentations 3 was in verses 31 and 32.

> For the Lord will not cast off forever. Though He causes grief, yet He will show compassion according to the multitude of His mercies.
>
> NKJV

That verse was like a light at the end of the tunnel for me. To know that things wouldn't be like this forever!

Though God had His hand in my injury, He would also show compassion. He had helped me through the long nights. He would be with me during the long days of adjusting to my wheelchair.

The yoke? Well, I'm no longer young, but it's still heavy to bear. Even so, time and again God in His grace has thrown out the sturdy lifeline of His Word just when I felt I was about to go under.

Look. There's a lifeline in front of you, too. Grab on — He'll never let you sink.

Wayside Interlude

By two utterly immutable things, the word of God and the oath of God, who cannot lie, we who are refugees from this dying world might have a powerful source of strength, and might grasp the hope that he holds out to us. This hope we hold as an utterly reliable anchor for our souls.

HEBREWS 6:18–19, PHILLIPS

The time to check your lifelines is before you enter a storm — not in the teeth of it. Even as a young, scared teenager, I had a few strong lifeline verses that kept me from being completely overwhelmed in my crisis. Now is the time to find, memorize, and meditate on some passages of Scripture that will be there for you when darkness is all around and the waves are breaking over your head.

DIRTY LAUNDRY

*I*magine you're coming back from a two-week trip with your suitcase stuffed with dirty laundry.

But somehow your luggage has been damaged in transit, and when you pick it up to head for the parking area, it suddenly flies open, dumping all of that laundry in the middle of a busy airport terminal.

And there you are, scrambling to pick up all of those items—dirty socks, soiled shirts, and rumpled unmentionables—before the curious eyes of passersby.

Not fun!

Our dirty laundry is for our eyes only. We don't want anybody else checking it out!

I think we sometimes feel the same way as believers. We catch ourselves hanging out a "laundered" version of the Christian life to attract unbelievers into the fold. We play down our problems, gloss over the hardships, throw a cover over the trials and tragedies, stuff our sorrows, and push all our weak or wounded brothers and sisters to the rear.

Oh, by all means, keep the dirty laundry stuffed in the suitcase or the laundry bag! Keep it undercover, where an observing world can't see. We don't want anyone thinking, *Look how this so-called loving God treats His devoted followers!*

And we certainly don't want the heartaches, depressions, divorces, and dissensions in our church to be ugly stains or embarrassing blotches against God's good name.

It's strange when you consider that our Lord Jesus did not seek to avoid the "dirty laundry" of His society. He actually sought out the company of prostitutes, outcasts, and indigents, apparently fearing no harm to God's reputation. He claimed responsibility for a man's blindness, put His arm around the leper, and gave special honor to the weak and the overwhelmed. While studiously avoiding the crisply laundered Pharisees, Jesus didn't seem embarrassed to hang out with the rumpled, the crumpled, and the stained.

There was this difference, however. The most obvious way God used suffering to glorify Himself back then was to miraculously *remove* it. Jesus went out restoring sight to the blind, healing to the lepers, life to the dead, and forgiveness to blatant sinners.

His ministry of healing and restoration captured lots of attention, for sure. Even when the unbelievers and scoffers saw the miracles, they marveled and glorified God.

But what about all the dirty laundry today? Jesus is no longer with us in bodily form, walking the hills of Judea, doing all the things He once did. Today, God has another way of using suffering to glorify Himself—a less obvious, but certainly not less powerful, way.

Strange as it may seem, and difficult as it may be to

accept, God often not only allows but actually ensures that you and I — His kids — undergo and endure long periods of difficulty, pain, and struggle.

And He lets all this take place within plain view of unbelievers!

But look what happens when these Christians on whom God has sent adversity after adversity refuse to complain. Look what happens when instead of cursing, complaining, and shaking rebellious fists at heaven, they respond with praise to their Creator.

Unbelievers take notice. They see something that, according to all the logical methods of accounting, simply doesn't add up. They are drawn to this God who inspires such loving loyalty from real people with real problems.

If you and I enjoyed nothing but ease and comfort, our world would never learn anything very impressive about God. It would never learn that God is *worth* serving — even when the going gets tough.

So let all those "pre-Christians" see what God is doing in your life. Let them identify with your dirty laundry. Don't hide your heartaches and areas of struggle, hypocritically pretending they don't exist. Instead, concentrate on staying loyal to your God in the midst of them.

It may be the most convincing argument your neighbors ever see or hear about the God you love.

Wayside Interlude

Be wise in the way you act toward outsiders; make the most of every opportunity. Let your conversation be always full of grace, seasoned with salt, so that you may know how to answer everyone.

COLOSSIANS 4:5–6

For unbelievers to see something attractive or compelling about your life and your faith, you have to be close to them. They won't notice or be moved by your walk with God if you never cross paths with them. Think through your upcoming week. At what points will you be close enough to men and women outside of Christ to engage them in conversation? Beyond that, what hobbies, classes, clubs, or endeavors could you join that would put you shoulder to shoulder with people who need Jesus? Then let them really see your life—even your dirty laundry.

WAITING

*G*od, are You there?

Silence.

Are You listening?

More silence.

Ummm…am I getting the idea that You're asking me to wait? Is that what I'm supposed to do? Just—sit here and WAIT?

A very long silence.

Why is it, God, that when I want to charge ahead, You insist I wait? And at other times—when I feel like waiting—You push me forward?

Deafening silence.

Ah, you had so hoped God wouldn't do this. Not now, not in this moment, not in this situation. But He has. And it's exasperating. He replies to your questions with long, drawn-out periods of silence. No answers. No direction. No warm fuzzies. No sign post pointing, "This is the way…walk ye in it." Just…waiting.

Okay. If I have to sit here and wait, then I'll…I'll…

Before you know it, you've created your own noise, activity, and excitement—anything but that grating stillness which seems to rub against the grain of your soul.

It's a common problem. We frantically crowd our time with more frenzy, hoping to satisfy our soul's longings. We do spiritual leapfrogs from one activity to the next…*leading a Bible study…organizing a potluck…working in the church nursery…teaching a Wednesday night class…etc., etc.*

And what does all this get us? Spiritual exhaustion. Mental burnout. Physical drain. And even a few more irksome feelings about God.

Oswald Chambers has observed, "When we are in an unhealthy state spiritually or emotionally, we always want thrills. And in the spiritual domain, if we insist on getting thrills, on mounting up with wings, it will end in the destruction of spirituality."

But I'm tired of waiting! you say. *Life is going by.*

Be at ease, my friend. The Spirit of Christ hasn't forgotten you or misplaced your file. Not for a heartbeat! He's totally engaged. He's listening. He cares more deeply than you could begin to comprehend.

Finally you heave a deep sigh. *I'm at the end of my rope. I yield to You, Lord.* And the Spirit goes to work. Ignoring your frenzy, bypassing your busyness, He elbows His way into your activity, whispering, *"Be still — cease striving! — and know that I am God."*

Even though you have a difficult time believing that any worthwhile activity can coexist with stillness, God begins to do His hushed work in your heart. He gives you His inexplicable calm as you wait by the hospital bed of your husband. He gives you His patience as you wait for the letter of acceptance from college. Peace as you wait for the first job opportunity. And more than that, He gives you Himself, His intimacy, as you search for answers to your deepest longings. It dawns on you that "rush" is wrong nearly every time.

It's a command; it's a charge: "Listen to me in silence...let the peoples renew their strength" (Isaiah 41:1, ESV).

It's a bidding, a mandate: "Be still before the LORD, all mankind" (Zechariah 2:13).

When we do, when we are — wonder of wonders! — we hear "a still, small voice." God's answer comes only through waiting.

> *Speak, Lord, in Thy stillness, while I wait on Thee;*
> *Hush my heart to listen in expectancy.*

Wayside Interlude

Wait for the LORD;
Be strong and let your heart take courage;
Yes, wait for the LORD.

PSALM 27:14, NASB

Are there margins of quiet in your life? Are there at least a few times in your day when all is quiet — no cell phone, no car radio, no iPod with headphones — and there's no one else around? If your life lacks "white space," if there is no space for the Lord to speak into the quietness of your thoughts, how will you hear Him? Could it be that He has been speaking to you just lately — steadily, lovingly, patiently — but you haven't heard Him through the noise?

Conclusion

*Y*ou've asked your good friend for directions. He obliges with a specific, detailed, hand-drawn map. Reassured, you set off on your journey only to discover the route he has given you is a jumbled mess. It's a nightmare of detours, potholes, puddles, ruts, and ripped-up pavement. Terrible drop-offs loom on the crumbling shoulders of the road, with no guardrail in sight. What's worse, there is nowhere to turn around—and you're much too far along to back up.

So there you are, bumping along with sharp-edged boulders knifing at your car's underbelly, and roadside brush clawing at the paint on the side of your car.

You'd be fuming, wouldn't you?

But what would hurt more than anything is the knowledge that your friend *knew* the road was like that. Most likely you'd pass the time rehearsing what to tell that so-called friend the next time you laid eyes on him.

"Hey, buddy, thanks for nothing! The next time I'll get where I need to go without your help!"

What would you think of a friend like that—one who had deliberately given you those directions and sent you down that dangerous road?

You'd drop him. Fast.

That's what you or I would do. Consider, though, what happened to the apostle Paul. The preacher from Tarsus was given directions that sent him down an even more tortuous road than the one I've just described—a road of dangers, hunger, humiliation, loneliness, pain, terror, and blood.

Paul had received his map—his trip directions—in the middle of the night in a lonely detention cell. And it wasn't even an angel who handed him the directions, it was the Lord Jesus Himself.

The following night the Lord stood near Paul and
said, "Take courage! As you have testified about
me in Jerusalem, so you must also testify in
Rome."

ACTS 23:11

Okay, so there was the Lord Jesus giving Paul his
route. "The road I want you to take, Paul, is the one that's
going to Rome. Keep heading in that direction no matter
what. You can't miss it."

With Jesus Himself as travel agent, you'd expect a
first-class trip, right? Not so. For two years on that long
road to Rome, Paul faced more than his fair share of
bypasses, ruts, hazards, and roadblocks. The journey fea-
tured constant trouble, murderous plots, and
imprisonments. Then there was the long detour when a
hurricane tossed him around the Mediterranean for four-
teen days.

Until his ship finally hit a sandbar.

And broke into pieces.

After which he managed to swim to an island.

After which he was bitten by a poisonous snake.

An easy road? Hey, the Roman Road was no freeway. The tolls were unbelievably high. And yet this was the very road Jesus *told* him to take! Ah, but Paul trusted his Friend. Though the road was rugged—even vicious at times—Paul trusted.

If the Lord Jesus had set him on the road to adversity, then he knew that, no matter what, it was the best road to heaven he could possibly find. No matter what happened to Him—smooth passage or storm—live or die—he was completely safe.

When I was younger in age—and younger in the faith—I would often hear older Christians speak about the "sufficiency of Christ"... "Christ and Christ alone"... "Jesus, Jesus, Jesus; sweetest name I know"... and how they knew nothing but "Christ and Him crucified."

I never said much about it (I wouldn't have dared!), but sometimes it seemed to me that these older believers were fixated on Jesus to the point of, well... spiritual myopia. It was too simple...too basic. There had to be more than just, you know...just Jesus.

But now, many years and miles down life's road from those days, I see what they mean. Christ and Christ alone? Yes. *Yes*. They were right.

After decades of living with quadriplegia (and encroaching pain on thin, tired bones), I have a radically different view of "overcoming adversity."

You may have never heard it expressed like this, but here it is: *To overcome adversity is to allow adversity to "overcome" you.* You allow those heartaches, pains, and perplexities to break apart the "rock of resistance" in your character, to lay you low, to humble you…so that you run—not walk, but RUN—to Jesus. In the shadow of His wings, in the safety of His arms, in the cleft of His rock, in the shelter of His fortress, in the hollow of His hand, I then find *safety*.

Proverbs 18:10 puts it this way, *"The name of the LORD is a strong tower; the righteous run to it and are safe."*

Safe.

I'm reminded of the old Fanny Crosby hymn:

Safe in the arms of Jesus, safe on His gentle breast
There by His love o'ershaded, sweetly my soul shall rest.

Safe in the arms of Jesus, safe from corroding care,
Safe from the world's temptations,
sin cannot harm me there.
Free from the blight of sorrow,
free from my doubts and fears;
Only a few more trials, only a few more tears!

And here are words I found just recently in an old
hymn I'd never sung before:

Safe home, safe home in port!
Rent cordage, shattered deck,
Torn sails, provisions short,
And only not a wreck;
But oh! the joy upon the shore
To tell our voyage—perils o'er!

The prize, the prize secure!
The athlete nearly fell;
Bare all he could endure,
And bare not always well;

But he may smile at troubles gone
Who sets the victor-garland on.

The exile is at home!
O nights and days of tears,
O longings not to roam,
O sins and doubts and fears;
What matters now grief's darkest day?
The King has wiped those tears away.

This is where I am living right now.

Just a moment ago, one of my dearest friends—who lost her husband three months ago—turned to me and said, "I love that word...*safety*."

It made me cry. It's the word I love most, too... it's what Jesus means to me more than ever.

Safe in Him. Christ and Christ alone. No matter what. Forever.

Also from
Joni Eareckson Tada

Sensitive reflections on the wonder of God's presence and encouragement for us to commune with Him regularly in the midst of our crazy, bustling world.

A Quiet Place in a Crazy World

Another "31 Days" title
from Joni

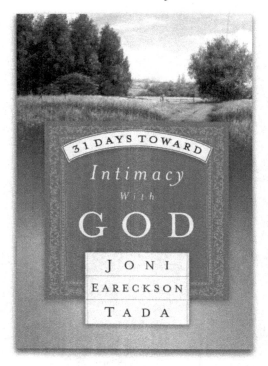

The more we get to know God, the more we will know life—the life we were created to experience. This devotional takes you on that journey!

31 Days Toward Intimacy with God

and Friends
The Disability Outreach of Joni Eareckson Tada

When a diving accident in 1967 robbed Joni of the use of her hands and legs, she found herself sequestered in a hospital ward, depressed and discouraged. Friends from her church rallied and offered help and practical assistance. Seeing how these friends made all the difference in her life, Joni gained a vision to help other churches across the country reach out to families like hers.

Now, almost 40 years later, Joni Eareckson Tada leads a worldwide team of skilled staff and volunteers through *Joni and Friends*, a Christian organization committed to accelerating ministry among families affected by disability. We are energized by the words of Jesus: "Go out and find the disabled and bring them in…so that my Father's house might be full" (Luke 14:13, 23).

If you are disabled, or know of a family affected by disability, we invite you to contact us for more information on our programs and outreach services:

The Joni and Friends International Disability Center
P.O. Box 3333
Agoura Hills, CA 91376
www.joniandfriends.org